LOCAL COUNCIL

Local Council Finance

Chris Richards and Ron Harrop

Shaw & Sons

Published by
Shaw & Sons Limited
Shaway House
21 Bourne Park
Bourne Road
Crayford
Kent DA1 4BZ

www.shaws.co.uk

© Shaw & Sons Limited 2002

Published June 2002

ISBN 0 7219 1580 9

A CIP catalogue record for this book is
available from the British Library

Printed in Great Britain by
Creative Print and Design (Wales), Ebbw Vale

CONTENTS

Contents

Contents

Contents

LIST OF TABLES

THE AUTHORS

Ron Harrop worked for the District Audit Service for many years, including a period as a Deputy District Auditor. He joined the Audit Commission when it was established in January 1983 and also served as a member of the CIPFA Higher Education Finance Executive. In 1988 he left the Audit Commission and became Finance Officer of Sevenoaks Town Council, where he stayed until his retirement.

Chris Richards is an accountant who has worked in the accountancy profession for more than 40 years, including several years in Africa. In 1996 he was asked by NALC to provide training for the then new Accounts and Audit Regulations. Ron Harrop assisted with the legal side and the training courses, which were held in London. The courses were also taken to many parts of the country and were attended by more than 1,000 delegates. He has for the last 10 years had his own accountancy practice.

PREFACE

This book is a sequel to *Parish, Town and Community Council Finance* written by Ron Harrop in 1992. Following the introduction of the Accounts and Audit Regulations 1996, local councils were, for the first time, required to produce accounts in a set format. Ron Harrop started to revise his text and in May 2001 I was asked to collaborate with him in completing this new book.

Ron Harrop was one of the team that produced the CIPFA Guide to the Regulations, which were 'Best Practice'. I first met Ron when the National Association of Local Councils ran a series of courses to introduce the new Regulations to clerks; he and I wrote and delivered the lectures during 1996.

The aim of this book is to provide a basic guide to the financial requirements of local councils. Experience has shown that the majority of local councils fall into the first two size bands, i.e. with an income of up to £500,000. Only 4% of councils are in the third band of over £500,000 income and, as the accounting requirements for that group are based on those for District Councils, which are much more complex, this book does not deal with that group.

I am indebted to my daughter, Judy Richards, for reading through the draft manuscript and suggesting areas which needed revision and simplification.

Chris Richards

INTRODUCTION

The accounting requirements for local councils have undergone great changes during the past five years, starting with the Accounts and Audit Regulations 1996, which introduced for the first time a standard format for the annual accounts. This climate of change is continuing with the introduction of a new approach to audits for 2001/02. This is a radical departure from previous practice; in most cases the auditor will not see the council's accounting records if the council can demonstrate that it has proper internal controls in place.

Further changes are likely to be brought in over the next few years as more professionally trained RFOs become available and the internal audit of each council is strengthened.

Any book can only deal with legislation at the time of going to print, so it is important that those responsible for councils' accounts watch carefully for changes in the future. These should be publicised in the journals of bodies such as the SLCC and NALC.

This book deals with the day to day accounting that a local council has to cope with and gives examples of the annual financial statements for councils in the two groups which have an income or expenditure of less than £500,000.

GLOSSARY OF ABBREVIATIONS

AAR   Accounts and Audit Regulations 1996

CIPFA   Chartered Institute of Public Finance and Accountancy

DEFRA   Department for Environment, Food and Rural Affairs

D of E Department of the Environment

DTLR   Department for Transport, Local Government and the Regions

NALC   National Association of Local Councils

PWLB   Public Works Loan Board

RFO   Responsible Financial Officer

SLCC   Society of Local Council Clerks

Chapter 1

ACCOUNTING REQUIREMENTS

Introduction

One of the most important tasks of the local council is to manage its finances. In order to do this efficiently, it is vital that accurate accounting records are maintained.

Councils are required to:

● Keep a record of receipts and payments.

● Keep records of assets and liabilities.

● Maintain measures to prevent and detect fraud.

● Identify the duties of all personnel who deal with financial transactions.

● Ensure that uncollected amounts, including bad debts, are only written off with the approval of the RFO, and for that approval to be shown in the accounting records.

The simplest form of accounting is the use of an analysed cash book, described in Chapter 4. This is the preferred accounting method for most small councils. Vouchers, invoices, etc. should be filed initially in an 'Unpaid' file; when paid, they should be transferred to a 'Paid' file. Larger councils may prefer to use a more sophisticated double entry system as their accounting requirements will naturally be more complex; this is dealt with in Chapter 6.

For all councils, the budget is the most important document. It is the master plan for the way a council uses its financial resources.

1

Financial Statements

Most people are familiar with the term 'Annual Accounts' – a statement which shows results for the financial year and often includes a balance sheet and notes. The current trend is to replace well known and easily understood expressions with jargon and thus 'accounts' have become 'financial statements'. In the majority of cases we have kept to the term 'accounts' in this book.

The financial statements are the responsibility of the council as a whole – not just the RFO or Chairman.

The financial statements must be made up to 31 March in each financial year and must be prepared in accordance with the Accounts and Audit Regulations 1996. These Regulations prescribe different requirements for each of the three different categories of council, based on income, as follows:

> Group A – Income over £500,000: detailed accounts based on those required for District Councils.

> Group B – Income between £50,000 and £500,000: Income and Expenditure basis.

> Group C – Income below £50,000: Receipts and Payments basis.

The Accounts and Audit Regulations 1996 lay down the minimum information to be shown in the accounts and the format to be used. The Annual Return includes a pro forma financial statement for completion. Councils are at liberty to include more information than is required by the Regulations, provided that the format laid down is adhered to.

It is permissible for a council to prepare accounts in accordance with the rules for a higher group – for instance a council with an income of £40,000 may wish to prepare accounts on an Income and Expenditure basis. Before 2001/02 the threshold between Groups B and C was £5,000 and many councils became accustomed to preparing their accounts under the Group B rules; some will continue to do so, even though it is not strictly necessary. Similarly, a number of councils whose income approaches the Group A threshold of £500,000 have opted to use the Group A format for their accounts.

Chapters 13 and 14 deal with the detailed format for the Annual Return of the Groups B and C in accordance with the *Governance and Accountability in Local Councils in England and Wales – A Practitioners' Guide* published by NALC and SLCC.

This book does not deal with the annual accounts for councils with an income of over £500,000.

Publication of Accounts

1. Prepare the accounts by 30th September.

2. The external auditor will set a date when local electors can ask questions about the accounts or object to an item in those accounts.

3. Display a notice in a conspicuous place that the accounts and other documents will be available for inspection for 15 full working days prior to the audit. At least 14 days' notice must be given, which means that the notice must be displayed at least 5 weeks prior to the audit.

   Tell the auditor that this has been done.

4. The accounts must be submitted to council for approval prior to the audit not later than 30 September. The

accounts submitted must be signed and dated by the Chairman and the Responsible Financial Officer (RFO – see Chapter 2) certifying that they present fairly the council's financial position.

5. The accounts must be made available for inspection for a period of 15 full working days prior to the audit, on receipt of reasonable notice.

6. When the audit has been completed, the accounts with attached notes and the audit opinion must be displayed in a conspicuous place for 14 days.

   Tell the auditor that this has been done.

7. If the audit has not been completed by 31 December:

   (a) the unaudited accounts must be displayed in a conspicuous place together with a statement explaining why the audit has not been completed;

   (b) when the audit is completed a notice must be displayed in a conspicuous place advising that the audit has been completed.

   Advise the auditor that this has been done.

8. Copies of the accounts must be made available for purchase at a reasonable price.

Computerisation

There are a number of computer programs available – some commercial programs and some specially designed for local councils. The principles described in this book apply equally to computer programs; the main difference is that the program deals with many of the mathematical and analytical tasks automatically.

Now that computers are relatively inexpensive and simple to use, many councils will decide to use one for accounting and other purposes (e.g. word processing). Remember that the following costs must be taken into account:

(a) hardware, purchase or lease price, maintenance and insurance;

(b) software, including that supplied annually for the update of budget changes;

(c) computer furniture, e.g. tables and storage cabinets;

(d) disks, tapes and computer stationery;

(e) staff time and training.

It is possible to buy basic computer hardware and all the necessary software to run accounts and payroll from around £1,000.

As software can, and should be, bought 'off the shelf', a major consideration is how a package will relate to other parts of the system, i.e. where will the input come from and what will the output be used for? These questions will be determined by cost and how far the system will be integrated into the other parts of the council's systems.

Charities and Trust Funds

Although the council may administer funds for charities or trusts, they are not part of the council's activities and do not form part of the council's accounts.

Separate accounts should be maintained and annual accounts drawn up in accordance with the Charity Commission rules.

Legislation

As legislation governing the way that local councils operate is constantly being revised, it is important to check that you have access to the latest information. SLCC and NALC keep their members informed of all changes and it is essential that all local councils belong to at least one of those bodies – and preferably both.

Chapter 2

THE RESPONSIBLE FINANCIAL OFFICER (RFO)

Under section 151 of the Local Government Act 1972, a local council is required to appoint an officer who is responsible for the administration of its financial affairs. That officer is known as the Responsible Financial Officer (RFO). The RFO is usually the Clerk but a different individual can be appointed to the post as is the case at some larger councils.

The Audit Commission expects that the RFO should be experienced in financial matters, and that a pool of competent RFOs should be available to all local councils. It is the duty of the RFO to determine the form and content of the council's accounts and supporting records, subject to any directions from the council and the provisions of the Accounts and Audit Regulations 1996. The RFO must ensure that the accounts and records are maintained in accordance with proper practices and are kept up to date (Regulation 4(1), Accounts and Audit Regulations 1996).

It is the council's responsibility to ensure that the following basic matters are in place:

1. The appointment of the RFO (section 151, Local Government Act 1972).

2. A definition of the RFO's duties (Regulation 4).

3. An adequate and effective system of internal audit (Regulation 5).

4. The year end final accounts – prepared and approved by the council by 30 September (Regulation 8).

If any of these basic requirements have not been met, the audit may not proceed until they are, and the auditor might seek an explanation from the Chairman.

Section 150(6) of the Local Government Act 1972 prescribed that every local council, and the Chairman of every parish meeting (for a parish not having a parish council), must keep such accounts as may be prescribed under that section, of the receipts and payments of the council or parish meeting as the case may be.

The RFO must ensure that the accounts are made up and ready for audit as soon as practicable and in any case not later than six months after 31 March (Regulation 8, Accounts and Audit Regulations 1996). Every officer employed by a local authority must also keep true accounts in writing of all money and property committed to his charge and render these accounts to the council as directed (section 25, Local Government Finance Act 1982).

Regulation 4(3) of the Accounts and Audit Regulations 1996 provides that the RFO's accounting records must contain the following:

(a) details of the sums of money received and spent by the council and the matters to which the receipts and payments (see Chapter 4) or the income and expenditure (see Chapter 5) accounts relate;

(b) a record of the assets and liabilities of the council;

(c) a record of income and expenditure in relation to claims made, or to be made, by the council for contribution, grant or subsidy from any Minister of the Crown.

Regulation 4(4) provides that the accounting control systems established by the RFO must include the following:

(a) measures to ensure prompt and accurate recording of financial transactions, measures to prevent and detect inaccuracies and fraud and the ability to reconstitute any lost records, e.g. computer back-up facilities;

(b) identification of the duties of officers dealing with financial transactions and division of responsibilities of those officers in relation to significant transactions;

(c) procedures for uncollectable amounts, including bad debts, not to be written off without the RFO's approval and for the approval to be shown in the accounting records.

The gist of the requirements set out in the two foregoing paragraphs should be included in financial regulations or, where a council is too small to have separate financial regulations, in standing orders.

Chapter 3

THE BUDGET

General

The importance of the annual budget cannot be over-emphasised. It forms a very important financial aspect of the Clerk's work and, where there is a separate finance officer, of his work too. It is their chief financial management tool. Its role as the foremost control mechanism in a council's financial affairs needs to be recognised and properly used.

Revenue

All local councils, except the very smallest, need an annual revenue budget. It is the master plan of the way in which a council intends to use its financial resources. Once it has been approved by the council, the budget becomes the authority for incurring the expenditure set out therein, and for regularly monitoring the income predicted. Without the expressed authority of the council, the limits on spending stipulated in the budget are not to be exceeded, nor should expenditure be incurred for purposes not included in the budget.

Local councils raise the bulk of the money necessary to meet their expenses by precept (a mandatory demand) issued on their District Council. Under the Council Tax legislation, the precept must be issued before 1 March each year, otherwise the local council is likely to incur penalties in relation to the dates on which the precept is paid. It is customary to submit the precept to the District Council Treasurer in late January or early February to enable him to prepare his District Council budget within the time limits. It should be noted, however, that this practice is only voluntary because statutorily the information does not have to be provided before the end of February. Under the Council Tax legislation, the precept covers the local council's needs for the ensuing financial year which, by law, runs from 1 April to the following 31 March for all local authorities. The District Council collects the amount precepted as part of the Council Tax levied on the Council Tax payers in the parish.

In order to establish the amount of the annual precept it is necessary to prepare a budget. The budget is a statement setting out item by item the purposes for which the council intends money to be spent during the financial year, showing the maximum amount which the council considers ought be spent for each purpose. It will also itemise the income likely to arise from the facilities provided by the council (such as cemeteries, village and community halls, recreation grounds, open spaces and allotments, etc.). In fixing a precept, it is best for a budget to be prepared for each committee at town councils and larger parishes with a final summary for use by the council (following a recommendation from its Finance Committee). Indeed such a practice should be (and usually is) laid down by those local councils.

At smaller parishes (i.e. the majority of cases) where there are no separate committee budgets, the budget goes straight to the council for consideration.

The difference between the total estimated expenditure and the total estimated income is the total estimated net expenditure, and is the basis for calculating the amount which must be raised by precept on the District Council.

Preparation of the Revenue Budget

At town councils and larger parishes the preparation of the annual budget commences, of necessity, in the previous

September so as to be in time for the precept to be fixed in January. In other parishes preparation should commence no later than November.

The first step in preparing the budget is to list all the heads under which the council is likely to have to spend money in the new financial year. The budget will certainly have to make provision for administration expenses – the cost of the clerk's salary, stationery, postage, telephone calls, hire of rooms for council meetings, etc. – and, depending on the scope of the council's activities, may go on to include provision for the upkeep and running of such things as a sports hall, a community centre, recreation ground, cemetery (see Table 3) and so on. In preparing the budget, care must be taken to allow for recurring charges such as rent, rates, instalments of loan repayments and interest on loans and telephone, gas and electricity charges, etc.

It helps greatly in estimating future spending if past experience can be used as a guide and many authorities adopt the practice of setting out their budgets with four columns side by side. Against each item is shown:

● the actual expenditure for the last completed financial year;

● the budget for the current financial year;

● the expected actual expenditure for the current financial year (i.e. the actual expenditure up to the date of the preparation of the budget plus the expected further expenditure in the period to the end of the current financial year);

● and, in the fourth column, the budgeted expenditure for the forthcoming year.

Income is similarly treated (see Tables 1 to 3 for town

councils and larger parishes and Table 4 for the smaller parishes).

The rate of inflation and changes in rates of pay and National Insurance must obviously be borne in mind and allowed for when preparing the budget. Regard must also be had to any expenditure in the current or previous year of an exceptional and non-recurring nature, for instance the purchase of a major item of equipment or the cost of a major scheme of repair work or improvement. The repayment of the final instalment of a loan will mean a reduction in the future level of expenditure. Similarly, the raising of a new loan will mean that estimates of future spending must be increased to allow for the annual payments of interest and instalments of principal in respect of the loan.

A decision by the council to curtail, end or increase an existing activity or to provide a new service or facility may well affect the pattern of spending. For instance, the provision of additional lamps for footway lighting will result in increased electricity bills, whilst a decision to open a sports hall or a community centre on more evenings or for longer hours will result in increased costs for heating, lighting and pay. A decision to acquire a piece of property or to erect a new building will not only affect the budget by way of increased loan charges (if money is borrowed for the purpose) but will require additional provision in the budget for the pay of a groundsman or caretaker and to meet the cost of maintenance and repairs.

Having estimated its probable expenditure, the council should then estimate its probable income from all sources, other than precept, using past experience as a guide and bearing in mind the likely effects of changes in any activity (e.g. the increase in income which should arise from the provision of a new tennis court or additional off-street parking facilities, and the diminution in income which would follow a decision to reduce the opening hours at a swimming pool).

Before the income budget is finalised all charges made by the council should be reviewed. It will not be practicable to increase them all every year, e.g. allotment rents, but, for example, those at sports halls and community centres should always be increased in line with increases in the pay of the staff who operate them. The same is true of cemeteries unless there are compelling reasons for not doing so.

Where a local council has appointed committees to manage its various services, each committee should formulate and put forward for approval its own part of the budget. Thus, the Open Spaces Committee will prepare that part of the budget related to the estimated expenditure on maintaining the parks, recreation grounds and cemetery, etc. and the estimated income from games in the parks, hire of pitches, burial fees, etc. Each committee's budget should then be incorporated in a single comprehensive budget statement for the consideration of the Finance Committee. Care must be taken to include in the overall budget provisions for expenditure on any purposes not falling within the jurisdiction of any other committee, such as administration expenses. Such expenditure and income should comprise the Finance Committee's budget.

On reviewing the overall position, the Finance Committee might conclude that some or all of the committee budgets were unacceptably high. It would then, according to the Committee's terms of reference as set out in standing orders, either amend them or refer them back to the spending committees indicating the extent and nature of the reductions in expenditure, or increases in fees and charges (to produce more income), which the Finance Committee felt were necessary.

Adjustments for Contingencies and Balances

However carefully and thoughtfully a budget is prepared, it is impossible to foresee every eventuality and councils should, and indeed are required by law to, make provisions in their budgeting for contingencies – events that may occur but for which there is no certainty. This is best done by making a separate provision in the budget so that the council is fully aware of the amount set aside to meet eventualities and can control its use. There should be no spending out of the contingency allowance without the approval of the council.

The difference between the total estimated expenditure (including the provision for contingencies) and the total estimated income will be the council's estimated net expenditure for the year. Before finally deciding that this is the amount for which it will precept, the council must have regard to the likely outcome of the current year's accounts. If they indicate that the current budget will be overspent, then a sum must be added on to the precept figure equivalent to the estimated amount of the overspending. If the indications are that the current budget will be underspent, then the amount of the precept should be reduced by the estimated underspending.

Councils should have a 'working balance', that is a sum carried forward each year to provide the funds for making payments in the interval from the beginning of each financial year to the date of the actual receipt of precept money from the District Council. The amount of the working balance should be reconsidered at budget time each year and, if the prevailing circumstances warrant an increase or a decrease in its amount, then the final precept sum should be adjusted by the necessary addition or deduction. Such an increase was required following the introduction of the Community Charge legislation. As a result of that legislation, the precept is payable in two instalments, one at the end of April and the other at the end of September. Because the first instalment is not payable until the end of April, the working balance must be sufficient to meet a whole month's payments, less any likely substantial income. That position has been perpetuated under the Council Tax legislation. In practice the payment of precepts varies. Some District Councils are more generous than most and give thought to the problems of their smaller parishes and pay the parish precepts in full in April. In some cases quite large sums are involved.

Formal Approval of the Budget

Finally, the budget should be formally approved and adopted by the council by resolution, and the same resolution could contain the necessary authority for the issue of a precept on the District Council for the amount required.

Examples of Budget Statements

There is no standard format laid down for a budget. The following Tables 1 to 3 show the type of budget commonly in use at town councils and larger parishes. The tables, which illustrate part of a revenue budget showing the final summary, a committee summary and part of that committee's detailed budget, should serve as a useful guide. They are in a form generally adopted by District Councils, etc.

Table 4 is an example of the form of a budget generally in use at smaller parishes.

The Budget

TABLE 1 – FINAL BUDGET SUMMARY

	Actual Previous Year	Budget Current Year	Probable Actual Current Year	Budget Next Year
Net Expenditure	£	£	£	£
Planning Committee	19,324	11,125	10,885	26,185
Open Spaces Committee	122,899	128,001	129,549	161,210
Finance Committee	57,751	98,396	98,328	109,200
Totals	199,974	237,522	238,762	296,595

Precept required for	£
Estimated total net expenditure (as above)	296,595
Add for: (a) contingencies	15,000
(b) working balance	35,000
	346,595
Less: Expected balance in hand at 31 March	45,527
Total precept required	£301,068
Say	£301,000

TABLE 2 – OPEN SPACES COMMITTEE

	Actual Previous Year	Budget Current Year	Probable Actual Current Year	Budget Next Year
Summary of Net Expenditure	£	£	£	£
1. Recreation grounds, Commons and Open Spaces	72,395	82,630	87,369	125,651
2. Cemetery (including closed churchyard)	50,282	45,151	41,951	35,359
3. Allotments	222	220	229	200
	122,899	128,001	129,549	161,210

17

TABLE 3 – CEMETERY AND CLOSED CHURCHYARD

	Actual Previous Year	Budget Current Year	Probable Actual Current Year	Budget Next Year
Expenditure	£	£	£	£
1. Pay and Allowances	30,600	33,000	32,425	35,500
2. Rates	925	975	1,210	1,390
3. Telephones	463	575	465	505
4. Lighting & Heating	126	325	440	500
5. Chapel Maintenance	8,463	500	455	1,100
6. Lodge Maintenance	—	3,500	3,100	3,500
7. Workshops/Garages	—	900	800	1,300
8. New Equipment	7,273	14,100	13,513	2,000
9. General Maintenance/ Servicing and Fuel	2,594	3,300	2,940	3,000
10. Trees, Plants, Turf and Fertilizer	2,160	2,000	1,224	2,000
11. Lawn/Wall of Remembrance	541	100	305	330
12. Roads and Paths	9,574	500	658	710
13. Fencing	—	500	200	200
14. Printing and Stationery	254	200	200	250
15. Sundries	492	500	220	—
Gross Expenditure	63,465	60,975	58,155	52,285
Income	£	£	£	£
16. Cemetery Receipts	12,559	15,200	15,580	16,250
17. House Rent	624	624	624	676
Gross Income	13,183	15,824	16,204	16,926
Net Expenditure	50,282	45,151	41,951	35,359

The Budget

TABLE 4 – BUDGET

	Actual Previous Year	Budget Current Year	Probable Actual Current Year	Budget Next Year
Expenditure	£	£	£	£
1. Administration	4,078	5,500	5,200	5,200
2. Planning	500	500	600	600
3. Sports Field	3,365	1,500	1,400	1,700
4. Play Scheme	1,701	2,000	2,100	2,200
5. Street Sweeping	1,140	1,300	1,400	1,400
6. Litter Bins	—	300	300	400
7. Aid to Village Hall	—	—	450	500
8. Footpaths & Signs	139	300	300	300
9. Grants	—	—	—	—
10. Section 137	—	—	—	—
11. Room Hire for Meetings	225	240	300	350
12. Neighbourhood Watch	75	100	100	100
13. Publicity	375	300	300	300
14. Jubilee Celebrations	—	300	300	—
15. Children's Play Areas	—	—	—	1,500
Gross Expenditure	11,598	12,340	12,750	14,550
Income	£	£	£	£
1. Administration	—	—	—	—
2. Sports Field	52	50	200	400
3. Play Scheme	1,708	1,800	1,900	2,000
4. Street Sweeping	1,157	900	1,146	1,200
5. Concurrent Functions Grant	6,666	3,500	4,193	3,220
6. Bank Interest	64	70	70	60
7. Miscellaneous	490	—	—	—
Gross Income	10,137	6,320	7,509	6,880
Net Expenditure	1,461	6,020	5,241	7,670

Continued overleaf

TABLE 4 (continued)
Precept required

		Budget Next Year £
Estimated total net expenditure (as above)		7,670
Add for: (a) contingencies		—
(b) working balance		1,500
		9,170
Less: Expected balances in hand at 31 March	5,000	
Less: Sports Field Renewals Fund	2,000	
		3,000
		6,170
Total Precept Required	*say*	£6,000

In this example, the council's cash balance includes a sum set aside for Sports Field Renewals, so this must be deducted from the cash balance.

Capital

So far we have talked about the revenue budget and there has been no reference to a capital budget. In this context the term 'capital' relates to the nature of the expenditure rather than the source from which it is financed, be it revenue, loan or special fund.

Capital expenditure is expenditure on the acquisition or construction of something (an asset) which will last for some years. Sometimes capital expenditure produces assets which are resaleable, e.g. purchases of land or construction of buildings. In other cases it produces something which is of lasting value to a local council but which is not resaleable, e.g. acquisition and erection of new children's playground, or repair and improvement of roads and footpaths in the cemetery.

Such work will involve much greater than normal expenditure and therefore it needs to be properly planned. Town councils and the larger parishes embarking on this work should have a long-term capital budget or rolling capital programme extending over, say, four years or the council's term of office following each election. Particular projects can then be brought forward, or put back, depending on the availability of funds and the speed with which the work progresses.

Soon after its inception, a new council should decide on a capital budget or programme to last over its four year term of office. Loan approvals (if required) can then be requested at the right time, enabling their effect on the revenue budget, and thus the precept, to be assessed. The capital budget should be reviewed from time to time as work progresses and any necessary changes made including the addition of new schemes and the deletion of existing ones. The capital budget must of course be reviewed at the time the annual revenue budget is being prepared and its likely effect on that budget over the coming financial year must be taken into account.

Chapter 4

THE CASH BOOK

Introduction

Before dealing with local council accounts themselves, it is necessary to understand certain basic accounting principles and conventions. This can best be done by explaining the operation of the primary account, the Cash Book, which is to be found in any accounting system. Every organisation has a Cash Book which records the transactions through its bank account.

Cash Book

Most smaller councils will keep an analysed cash book, such as those produced by Shaw & Sons Ltd. In local council terms 'cash' includes both cash and bank/building society accounts.

The cash book records on the left-hand (debit) side moneys received and on the right-hand (credit) side monies paid out.

Whenever it is necessary to ascertain the balance of cash in hand or overspent – for example, in order to report the financial position at any time to the council, or to complete the accounts at the end of the financial year – both sides of the account are added up. A figure known as the 'balance' is then inserted and added on to the side of the account with the smaller total to make its total equal to that of the other side. If the balance has to be inserted on the 'credit' or payments side of the account, then it represents the amount which is in hand, for at that date the total receipts exceed the total payments by that amount. Conversely, if the balance has to be inserted on the 'debit' or receipts side of the cash account, then it represents the amount which is overspent, because at that date the total payments exceed the total receipts.

When the account is ruled off and balanced, the balance must be carried forward to the new accounting period. If the balance appears on the 'credit' or payments side, it should be carried forward and entered on the other side (the 'debit' or receipts side) of the account for the succeeding period. The balance represents the amount of money in hand available for spending along with any other moneys received in the new accounting period. If the balance appears on the 'debit' or receipts side when the account is ruled off, then it must be carried forward and entered on the 'credit' or payments side of the account for the succeeding period along with the payments to come in the new period. The overspending must be met out of receipts at some point in the future.

Tables 6 and 7 at the end of this chapter show examples of the receipts and payments sides respectively of the Cash Book.

Form of the Cash Book

Every entry in the Cash Book of either a receipt or a payment should show the following particulars:

(a) date money received or paid;

(b) from whom received, or to whom paid;

(c) nature of the receipt or the payment;

(d) a serial numerical reference to the relevant receipt or, in the case of a payment, reference to the appropriate invoice – the receipt, or payment vouchers; the cheque numbers should also be entered;

(e) the amount of the receipt or payment and the amount of VAT included (if any) in each receipt or payment;

(f) analysis columns so that the net payment/receipt can be analysed – usually under budget headings. The first column will be headed 'Total' and the second column is 'VAT'; other columns should be added as required to record transactions for the various activities of the council (see below).

The entry describing the receipt or the payment under head (c) above need only be brief; for example, in the case of the receipt of money the following would suffice:

- 'precept';
- 'allotment rent';
- 'burial fee';
- 'Investment interest;
- 'rent', etc.;

and in the case of payments:

- 'Clerk's salary';
- 'stationery';
- 'pavilion repairs';
- 'business rates';
- 'tractor fuel', etc.

The reference number quoted under head (d) should, in the case of money received, be the serial number of the receipt voucher and, in the case of payments, the suppliers' invoices and other supporting documents which are being paid and should be marked with a serial number.

These suggestions will help ensure that no item is overlooked and help with the subsequent reconciling of the account.

The Cash Book should be entered up (posted) regularly so as to avoid confusion and waste of time in the future. After numbering and posting, the receipt vouchers and the payment vouchers should be neatly filed away. On no account should they be left lying around unposted for weeks or months on end.

Analysis Columns

The analysis columns of the council should only record transactions net of Value Added Tax.

Apart from the Total and VAT, column headings should include:

● receipts and payments relating to allotments;

● each charity or trust of which the local council is the trustee;

● receipts and payments on a loan account;

● payments under section 137 of the Local Government Act 1972 as amended by section 36 of the Local Government and Housing Act 1989 (a useful guide to section 137 is published by the Hampshire Association of Local Councils);

● receipts and payments relating to any purpose (e.g. footway lighting) the cost or benefit of which is chargeable to, or accrues to, part only of the council's area;

● transactions relating to any fund established under Schedule 13 of the Local Government Act 1972, i.e. a renewals and repairs fund, a capital fund or a loans fund;

● payments relating to publicity under section 5 of the Local Government Act 1986;

- receipts and payments for the main budget heads, e.g. Parks, Community Hall, Street Lighting, Burial Ground.

Check that you have the appropriate columns for your council.

An example of an analysed cash book is shown in Tables 6 and 7 at the end of this chapter.

Bank Accounts

Every local council, however small, should have a bank account. Moneys received by officers on behalf of the council should be banked in the council's account as soon as possible, and all payments, except small petty cash items, should be made by cheque drawn on the council's account. The maximum security is thus provided for the council's funds.

In the case of small parish councils, banks often make no charge for operating their accounts provided there is no over-drawing. As to larger local councils, agreement should be reached with the local bank manager that bank charges will not be levied provided a minimum balance is maintained in the account.

Where a charge is made it will be related to the number of entries made in the account each quarter, plus interest if the account is overdrawn. Banks are in competition with each other for business and it is for each local council to see which of the local banks can offer the best terms.

Bank Statements

Bank statements are a very necessary aid to the Clerk in checking the accounts and in bringing to light and correcting any errors that may have occurred. Obviously a bank statement must be obtained at 31 March each year so that the balance at the end of the financial year can be verified and agreed. During the course of the year all but the smallest local councils should obtain statements monthly. On receipt, they should be checked and reconciled with the Cash Book. Failure to do this can lead to a tedious time-wasting search for errors which occurred some time ago.

This checking must be done carefully so as to identify each item, referring to cheque and paying-in stubs as necessary. There is no need for the bank to return the paid cheques, a practice which has long ceased to operate in the commercial world and with personal accounts. Should there be a query by a creditor, the banks will always produce proof of payment, if in fact it has been made. Naturally the banks will charge for the additional service of returning paid cheques. It is therefore a waste of the council's money, the Clerk's time, and also storage space.

Reconciliation of Cash Book Balances with Bank Balances

It is often the case that the balance on the bank statement at a given date does not agree with the balance in the Cash Book at the same date. It is necessary therefore to establish the reason for the difference and ascertain whether there are any errors in either the Cash Book or the bank statement. There are a number of circumstances, other than error, which can cause such a difference. Such differences should be recorded in writing in a 'Bank Reconciliation Statement'. Two of the most common relate to unpresented or 'outstanding' cheques and receipts which have been banked but have not yet appeared on the bank statement.

Entries in a Cash Book in respect of payments made by cheque should record the dates on which the cheques were drawn and signed. Obviously, the cheques will not find their way to the bank for payment until some time later and, accordingly, their payment will be recorded in the bank statement at later dates. If these later dates extend beyond the date on which the accounts are balanced, the bank balance will be inflated to the extent of those 'outstanding' cheques. Such cheques should be recorded in the bank reconciliation statement and deducted from the bank balance so as to agree with the Cash Account balance. Careful comparison and marking off of the payments recorded in the Cash Account with those in the bank statement will reveal how many such cheques there are.

The second most common instance for which an adjustment may have to be made is in respect of moneys which the Clerk or RFO may have received just before the date of balancing but which it has not been possible to bank until later. In these circumstances the balance on the bank statement is obviously too low to the extent of the receipts not appearing on it. This money must be recorded in the reconciliation statement and added to the bank account balance so as to agree with the Cash Book balance.

Some large local councils may use more than one bank account in conjunction with their Cash Book. For example, a council may keep some of its funds in a bank deposit account, or may invest surplus funds on a longer term basis in, say, a high interest bank account, a building society or a national savings investment account. A council may also operate a separate bank account out of which all payments are made and which is kept in funds by transfers from the main bank account; this is called an 'Imprest' account. The council may operate a separate wages and salaries bank account out of which the staff are paid by cheque or through the BACS system, and which is similarly kept in funds by transfers from the main bank account.

In such cases the bank reconciliation statement will be

more complicated. Care must be taken to include the balances on all the bank accounts and to allow for transfers between accounts (particularly from Post Office Giro accounts) which have not been fully effected in both accounts at the date of balancing. It is preferable to keep a separate Cash Book for each account, as this makes reconciliation much simpler.

Table 5 gives an outline of a bank reconciliation statement showing the entries which would be necessary to take account of all the circumstances that would cause differences, quite properly, between Cash Book and bank account balances.

TABLE 5 – BANK RECONCILIATION

Reconciliation of balances at 31 March 20**

Balances per Bank Statements
Current a/c ....
Deposit a/c ....
Salaries Imprest a/c ....
_____
....

Less: Unpresented Cheques
1234 ....
1235 ....
1236 ....
_____
....
_____
....

Add: Deposits not yet credited on
Bank Statement ....
....
_____ ....
_____
Balance per Cash Book £ ....
_____

29

Unpresented Cheques

Cheques which, at the end of six months from the date of issue, have not been presented (i.e. cleared through the council's bank account) should be cancelled and written back. Banks will normally not honour a cheque which is more than six months old but, to be on the safe side, the bank should be notified in writing of the serial number, name of payee and the amount of any cheque which is six months old, with instructions not to honour it. Out-dated cheques are written back by a simple entry on the receipts (debit) side of the Cash Book, recording that the entry is in respect of the writing back of a cancelled unpresented cheque and giving the cheque serial number and payee and, in the cash column, the amount of the cheque. The effect of this action is to cancel (or 'contra') the original entry on the payments side of the account and no other entries are required. Should the creditor at some future date reassert his claim, then a fresh cheque should be drawn and the second payment recorded in the Cash Book.

Overdrafts

It is important that members know and are aware of the full extent of their council's liabilities and that they take sensible precautions to prevent fraudulent manipulation of the council's funds. To this end, a council's Financial Regulations should provide that the council's bank account must not be overdrawn without the express authority of the council given in writing; and the bank must be made aware of this prohibition.

There can be times and occasions when it is proper for a council to incur a bank overdraft, for example in order to pay for some preliminary or early work on a project prior to the raising of the loan which it is empowered to borrow, or to meet urgent expenditure for which provision has not

30

been made in the current precept or precept instalment from the District Council. This latter situation suggests, however, that the sum set aside for contingencies is insufficient and needs reviewing at the next budget. The usual practice is for the council to pass a resolution (on the advice of the Finance Committee) instructing the Clerk or RFO to negotiate with the bank overdraft facilities not exceeding a stated sum for a specified period. A copy of the resolution, signed by the Chairman, must be sent to the bank.

Where an officer of the council is entrusted with moneys to be used to pay salaries and wages or petty cash expenses and the amounts entrusted to him are sizeable, it is essential to open a special bank account for his use. The officer must be told that under no circumstances must he overdraw on this account and the bank must be given explicit instructions in writing that no overdraft must be allowed and that the council will not be responsible for any overdraft.

Cash Flow

Local councils should not maintain unnecessarily large credit balances in their current accounts as these do not normally earn interest. Any surplus should be transferred to at least a bank deposit account where it can earn interest for the council. Where the surplus is sizeable, say £10,000 or over, a higher rate of interest can be earned by investing for a previously agreed fixed term, usually 1, 2 or 3 months, in a higher interest rate bank account or with a building society. Interest rates need to be kept under review to ensure that the maximum amount of interest is earned.

Arrangements for transfers between a council's current and deposit accounts can be made on instructions given by letter signed by the Clerk and/or the RFO. Transfers to a building society are usually made through the bank's computerised transfer system by means of an order signed by the Clerk and/or the RFO. Transfers back from a building society are arranged over the telephone and confirmed by letter from the building society. All this facilitates ease of operation and enables the Clerk or RFO to make transfers to and from accounts as necessary, maintaining only sufficient funds in the current account to meet cheques actually drawn and sent out, plus any direct debits. This requires care and some skill with a close watch being kept on the cash balance, otherwise the bank account could become overdrawn and interest and bank charges incurred. The bank statements for the current and deposit accounts should be carefully compared as soon as they are received to ensure that the date and amount of every transfer between the accounts has been accurately recorded in both accounts.

The amount of any interest received must be entered on the receipts (or debit) side of the Cash Book. Failure to record the interest received in the Cash Book is common but the omission will be revealed when the bank and Cash Book balances are reconciled.

The Council Tax legislation has severely restricted the amount of interest which can be earned through investing the precept until it is required. Whereas previously the precept was paid in full in April, often on 1 April, under current legislation half is paid on 30 April and the other half by 30 September. The second instalment can, however, be paid earlier at the discretion of the District Council, if for instance it considers there will be sufficient funds in the Council Tax collection account to enable it to do so.

Under section 353 of the Income and Corporation Taxes Act 1970, local authorities, including local councils, are exempt from Income Tax, Corporation Tax and Capital Gains Tax and therefore steps should be taken to make quite sure that investment interest is received gross. There is no problem with National Savings investment interest as it is always paid gross but care is needed with banks and building societies as their normal practice is to pay interest net of tax.

From the basic Cash Book, the Receipts and Payments Account can be produced. An example is given in Chapter 13.

TABLE 6 – CASH BOOK RECEIPTS

Date 20**	From whom received	Details	Voucher No.	Gross	VAT	Precept	Open Spaces	Sports Centre	Establishment	Cemetery	Allotments	Tourist Info.	Sundry	Opening Balance
May														
1	Totals b/f from April			12,504.63	362.44		352.61	3,020.15	16.00	365.00	35.00	153.19		8,200.24
1	XY District Council	Precept instalment	25	8,000.00		8,000.00								
3	B. Woods	Rec. ground receipts	26	56.40	8.40		48.00							
3	A. Robic	Sports centre course fees	27	2,483.34	369.86			2,113.48						
4	Scrubbers Cricket Club	Rent of cricket pitch	28	150.00			150.00							
8	Women's Institute	Hire of Committee room	29	8.00					8.00					
10	B. Woods	Rec. ground receipts	30	65.69	9.78		55.91							
10	A. Robic	Sports centre course fees	31	981.12	146.12			835.00						
14	A. Coffin & Co. Ltd.	Cemetery fees	32	110.00						110.00				
17	Badminton Club	Court hire	33	60.00				60.00						
17	L.E.O. Tard	Gym classes	34	173.70	25.87			147.83						
18	A. Coffin & Co. Ltd.	Cemetery fees	35	85.00						85.00				
22	Chippings and Co.	Memorial fees	36	55.00						55.00				
24	A.H.A.	Allotment rents	37	25.00							25.00			
25	Building Society	Investment interest	38	2,132.06									2,132.06	
29	Customs & Excise	VAT refund (March)	39	1,039.42									1,039.42	
29	Tourist Information Centre	Sales	40	109.90								109.90		
		TOTALS		28,039.26	922.47	8,000.00	606.52	6,176.46	24.00	615.00	60.00	263.09	3,171.48	8,200.24

The Cash Book

TABLE 7 – CASH BOOK PAYMENTS

Date 20**	To whom paid	Details	Voucher No.	Gross	VAT	Open Spaces	Sports Centre	Establishment	Cemetery	Allotments	Tourist Info.	Planning	Investments	Payroll Transfers
May														
1	P Books & Co	Sale goods – tourist information centre	149	210.27							210.27			
1	Cash	Petty cash reimbursement	150	82.41	5.19	77.22								
2	Caxton & Co Ltd	Printing sports centre programme	151	152.75	22.75		130.00							
2	W Paling & Co	Repairs to allotment fencing	152	409.56	61.00					348.56				
2	Building Society	Investment deposit	153	6,000.00									6,000.00	
3	XY District Council	Business rates	154	897.45			206.24	402.31	73.55		215.35			
8	Electricity Board	Electricity	155	730.10	108.73	72.32	141.42	197.71	65.69		144.23			
8	Horizontal Trees Ltd	Tree surgery	156	1,245.99	185.57	1,060.42								
8	British Telecom	Telephone	157	608.89	90.68	33.82	55.92	256.89	33.89		137.69			
8	A R Bishop Ltd	Repairs to cemetery chapel roof	158	4,700.00	700.00				4,000.00					
15	Gutterpress Chronicle	Advertising planning committee meetings	159	129.25	19.25							110.00		
15	Push Start Motors	Tractor, truck and mower fuel	160	218.77	32.58	161.03			25.16					
15	Neverclose Theatre	Donation	161	400.00				400.00						
17	Salaries and wages		162	1,000.00										1,000.00
22	Fotoqik	Photocopier rental	163	152.75	22.75			130.00						
22	Post Office	Tractor licence	164	16.10		8.05			8.05					
22	Rapid Erecting Ltd	Hire of scaffolding	165	1,175.00	175.00			1,000.00						
22	Re-cyclers Ltd	Office stationery	166	147.11	21.91			89.07			36.13			
				18,276.40	1,445.41	1,412.86	533.58	2,475.98	4,206.34	348.56	743.67	110.00	6,000.00	1,000.00
		Closing balance		9,762.86										
				28,039.26										

35

Chapter 5

INCOME AND EXPENDITURE ACCOUNTING

Introduction

Chapter 4 describes the basic Cash Book which records receipts and payments. Smaller councils will be able to prepare their annual accounts from this.

Councils with an income over £50,000 are required to prepare their financial statements on an Income and Expenditure basis. This takes account of income that is receivable during the year, whether or not it has been received and expenditure that is incurred, even though it may not have been paid for.

Income and expenditure accounting makes it easier to effect comparisons with the council's budget and therefore demonstrate how successfully the council is keeping within the budget. This is particularly so at the end of a financial year. Under receipts and payments accounting, payments relating to one financial year, if made in the next financial year, will be recorded in that financial year, although provided for in the previous financial year's budget. However, under income and expenditure accounting such payments will be recorded in the correct financial year. Conversely, the same applies to the late payment of money due to the council.

Finally, it is essential for a council's general fund balance (and for that matter any other fund balances) to be recorded correctly. This is particularly important in helping to ensure that the precept, and therefore the Council Tax, are no greater than they should be. Unlike receipts and payments

36

accounting, the amount of the year-end balance does not depend on whether creditors present their bills and debtors pay what they owe before or after 31 March.

The practice of incorrectly dating batches of cheques near the end of March, when in fact they are not drawn until April, is to be discouraged as this produces a long list of unpresented cheques at 31 March. It is sometimes adopted so as to record the payments in the financial year for which they have been budgeted and/or to use up an underspent budget whilst still maintaining receipts and payments accounting. If it comes to the notice of the auditor, it will at the very least attract adverse criticism from him.

The Principles

Income and expenditure accounting is based on the principle of double-entry book-keeping, which recognises and records the fact that every transaction has two aspects – the giving of a benefit and the receiving of that benefit. Each transaction, therefore, must be entered twice in the accounts; once in the account receiving the benefit and once in the account giving the benefit. The account that receives a benefit is always debited (that is, the transaction is recorded on the left-hand side of the account); the account that gives the benefit is always credited (that is, the transaction is recorded on the right-hand side of the account).

For example, in compliance with an order of the council, a firm (W. Paling & Co.) supply and erect a length of fencing at the council's allotments. This transaction involves the giving of a benefit by W. Paling & Co. and the receiving of the benefit by the council's allotments. It would be recorded by crediting the Cash Account (the account which gave the benefit) when Paling & Co.'s invoice was paid, and debiting the Allotments Expenditure Account (the account which received the benefit), as follows:

Cash Account			**Allotments Account**		
Dr		Cr	Dr		Cr
	W Paling	100	W Paling, fencing	100	

Income and expenditure accounting is obviously more complex than receipts and payments accounting and requires the keeping of a number of different subsidiary accounts. A list of those which are required to record the usual transactions of a local council is as follows:

Cash Account

Debtors' Accounts

Creditors' Accounts

Payroll Accounts

Income Accounts and Expenditure Accounts

Revenue (or Fund) Accounts

Loan and Capital Accounts

Capital Receipts Accounts.

The transactions to be recorded in each of the foregoing accounts are discussed in the following paragraphs. The nature of the transactions to be recorded will determine the number of accounts that are required.

The Accounting Records

Smaller councils may find that it is possible to use an analysed cash book and make adjustments at the year end on separate working papers. The subsidiary records such as allotment rents and debtors can be maintained in separate files.

Those councils that have a higher income will find that it is necessary to keep the records on a double-entry system. This requires a basic knowledge of double-entry book-keeping.

Most computer programs can be used without a knowledge of double-entry book-keeping, although any accounting knowledge will always be useful. Some of the smallest councils use computers – it is the clerk's choice to use whichever method he is comfortable with.

Cash Account (or Cash Book)

Remember that in local government parlance the term 'cash account' includes cash, bank and building society accounts.

The Cash Account should record the details of all moneys received on behalf of the council and all payments made on its behalf; a detailed explanation of the operation of a Cash Account, together with a worked example, is given in Chapter 4. A Cash Account can take the form of a computerised record, a spreadsheet or a manual record such as the 'old fashioned' receipts and payments account.

Debtors' Accounts

The Debtors' Account records sums of money (debts) due to the council and payments received in respect of those debts, and the balance outstanding at any time:

● debts due must be entered on the debit (left-hand) side of the account; and

● receipts in discharge of those debts are recorded on the credit (right-hand) side of the account.

The difference between the respective totals of the two sides at any date represents either:

(a) the amount still owed to the council if the debits exceed the credits; or

(b) the amount overpaid or paid in advance by the debtors if the credits exceed the debits.

All invoices sent out should be debited to a Debtors' Account for a named person or body (in those cases where there is a regular series of transactions with the same person or body), or for a particular group of like debtors, for example, allotment tenants.

The debits to the Debtors' Account are usually cross-referenced to the various Income Accounts which have been correspondingly credited; and the credits are cross-referenced to the corresponding debits in the Cash Account. As with the Cash Account, Debtors' Accounts can be computerised or manual.

If it appears at any time that a debt or part of a debt is irrecoverable, the authority of the council or the Finance Committee of the council should be obtained to write it off. That amount should then be deleted from the accounts by crediting the Debtors' Account and debiting the appropriate Income Account with the sum involved under the description of 'written off as irrecoverable' and signed by the RFO, giving reasons for the write-off.

Creditors' Accounts

The Creditors' Account records amounts owed by the council to its creditors as a general body and records the payments made by the council in satisfaction of its debts.

Local authorities normally pay their bills as they are

received so it is not general practice to set up Creditors' Accounts for bills received during the year, thus saving time and effort. As they are paid, the bills are credited to the Cash Account and debited to the appropriate Expenditure Account.

However, those bills which it has not been possible to pay by 31 March – the end of the financial year – must be credited to a Creditors' Account and debited to Expenditure Accounts as appropriate. The value, or estimated value, of goods or services received but not invoiced by 31 March should also be credited to the Creditors' Account and debited to the appropriate Expenditure Accounts. When payment is made, the Cash Account is credited and the Creditors' Account debited.

Where the estimated value of goods and/or services received has been entered in the accounts and the amount eventually paid is different, it will be necessary to make an adjustment between the Creditors' Account and the relevant Expenditure Account.

In this way the council's commitments are brought fully to account and their effect on the council's financial position shown more accurately. For the larger local council this is an important benefit compared to receipts and payments accounting, particularly in a climate of close scrutiny.

Payroll Accounts

For councils with a significant number of employees, wages and salaries should be paid from a separate account funded from the main bank account from time to time by lump sum transfer. For convenience, payments can then be made by cheques requiring one signature only.

The operation of the payroll is discussed in Chapter 9.

Income Accounts and Expenditure Accounts

Income Accounts and Expenditure Accounts, as their names imply, are accounts which bring together respectively all the council's expenditure or all the council's income relating to particular purposes, functions or services. At the end of each financial year the totals of Income Accounts and Expenditure Accounts are transferred to the appropriate Revenue or Fund Account.

There must be at least the minimum number of separate Income Accounts and Expenditure Accounts to comply with the statutory or other requirements regarding the keeping of separate accounts for certain purposes. For example, separate accounts must be maintained for payments under section 137 of the Local Government Act 1972.

In addition there can be as many Income Accounts and Expenditure Accounts as are necessary for a particular local council's purposes, e.g. playing fields and village halls, as shown in the budget heads.

Items of expenditure are debited to Expenditure Accounts, the corresponding credits being either to the Cash Account or to the Creditors' Account. Items of income are credited to Income Accounts, with the corresponding debits being either to the Cash Account (cash receipts) or to Debtors' Accounts (where bills have been sent out).

At the end of the financial year, each Expenditure Account is totalled and a sum equal to the balance is entered on the credit side of the account with the notation, as appropriate, 'transferred to General Revenue Account'. Each Income Account is similarly totalled at the end of the financial year, entering the balance on the debit side as a transfer to the credit of the appropriate Revenue Account. See below for an example of an Expenditure Account.

TABLE 8 – EXPENDITURE ACCOUNT

Parks Running Cost Account

Dr				Cr
Dec	Repairs	650	Mar Tfr to Gen	
Jan	Groundsman	250	Revenue A/c	1,125
Feb	Fencing	100		
Mar	Mowing	125		
		£1,125		£1,125

Revenue (or Fund) Accounts

Revenue or Fund Accounts are those to which the totals of their respective Income Accounts and Expenditure Accounts are transferred at the end of a financial year. Transfers from Income Accounts are credited (entered on the right-hand side), whilst transfers from Expenditure Accounts are debited (entered on the left-hand side). Revenue or Fund Accounts also record the balances (surplus or deficit) brought forward from the previous financial year. A 'surplus' balance brought forward will appear on the credit (right-hand) side of the account, a 'deficit' balance brought forward will appear on the debit (left-hand) side of the account.

TABLE 9 – GENERAL REVENUE ACCOUNT

Dr			Cr
Admin	65,382	Precept	80,500
Parks	6,248	Community Hall	5,843
Sports Field	13,276	Sports Field	15,384
Highways	14,376		
	99,282		101,727
Surplus for year	2,445	Balance Brought	
Balance Carried		Forward	35,917
Forward	35,917		
	£137,644		£137,644

When all the transfers for a year have been completed, both sides of a Revenue or Fund Account are totalled (including any balance brought forward) and a new balance between the totals of the two sides of the account is struck. If the balancing figure has to be entered on the debit side of the account to make it equal to the credit side, then that balance represents a surplus carried forward, because the income has exceeded the expenditure. Alternatively, if the balancing figure has to be entered on the credit side of a Revenue or Fund Account, then it represents a deficit, because the expenditure has exceeded the income.

Income and expenditure relating to specific funds that the council has set up, e.g. Community Hall Repairs Fund, are transferred to the General Fund Account and a transfer is made in the annual accounts from the General Fund to the specific fund account.

Year End Adjustments

At the year end it will be necessary to make adjustments for income and expenditure that is reflected in the wrong year. Adjustments made the previous year should be reversed.

Income

Income that is due but not received at 31 March should have been dealt with in the Debtors Ledger but there will always be other items to be adjusted such as deposits received for hall bookings in the following year or licence fees that cover more than one year. These will have to be excluded from the current year and carried forward. Remember to bring forward the previous year's adjustments so as to reflect the true income for the year.

Expenditure

If the council's system is based on cash transactions only, it will be necessary to bring into account all suppliers' invoices that are unpaid at the year end; these should be allocated to the appropriate expense head. Expenses that relate to the year but cannot at this stage be accurately quantified should be *accrued*, that is, a provision should be included for the estimated amount of the expense. An example of this type of adjustment is the audit fee; the audit for the current year will not be billed for some months after the year end so the amount can only be estimated based on the previous bill.

Materiality

With all accounts adjustments, only those adjustments that are material should be made. For councils with an income in excess of £50,000, no adjustment of less than £100 should be made as the value is insignificant in relation to the level of activity.

For regular utilities costs such as rent, telephone, electricity or water, there is no need to make any adjustments provided that there is included a full year's charge, e.g. four quarterly bills or two half yearly bills.

The Balance Sheet

Whilst a Balance Sheet is not required under the Regulations, larger councils may wish to prepare one. The Balance Sheet is the final statement which rounds off the accounts at the end of the financial year. Quite simply it brings together all the closing balances on the council's accounts at 31 March. It is arranged in such a way that it shows the financial position of the council at that date; the assets (excluding capital assets) less liabilities represents the net worth of the council which is represented by the total funds – General, Capital and Earmarked.

An example of the accounts is given in Chapter 14.

Chapter 6

INTERNAL CONTROL AND INTERNAL AUDIT

Internal Control

Many local councils employ at most a part-time Clerk and perhaps the occasional other part-time employee. This leaves little scope for internal check and, until the Accounts and Audit Regulations 1996, there was none at all for internal audit.

It is the RFO's responsibility to ensure that proper internal controls are set up and adhered to. These controls must ensure that:

1. Income and expenditure are in accordance with budgets.

2. All income that is due is actually received.

3. Expenses have been properly authorised before being paid.

4. The books of account are maintained on a regular basis and are regularly reconciled.

It falls on the council members to exercise a reasonable degree of control over financial matters. Prior to cheques being signed, invoices and other supporting documents will, of course, be carefully scrutinised against the list for payment submitted at the council or Finance Committee. The Clerk should produce a monthly statement to the appropriate meeting, showing the council's bank balances, etc., and a statement showing the council's detailed budget compared with the income and expenditure or the receipts and payments to date. An example of such a statement is

47

set out at the end of this chapter. It is intended for larger councils but is suitable for adaptation to meet the needs of smaller councils.

At the larger local councils with a full-time Clerk and perhaps a full-time or part-time RFO and other staff, it will be possible to establish some internal check.

For example, when dealing with invoices, one person should check and code them, another should authorise them for payment, and a third person should prepare the cheques for signature and analyse and post the invoices in the Cash Book. When working out salaries or wages, one person should calculate the gross pay from the pay register and/ or certified timesheets, and another should calculate the net pay and prepare the BACS transfer form for signature and submission to the council's bank on the required day.

For smaller councils, one or more of the members should undertake routine checks to ensure that the account books are being kept properly.

The controls required include:

- checks to ensure that the cash book (and any other accounting records) are being correctly written up and are mathematically correct;

- checks that the bank reconciliation is done regularly;

- checks to ensure that all income due is actually received;

- checks that the financial statements produced to council agree with the accounting records.

These are reasonable controls about which no one can complain. However, members should be careful not to interfere with their Clerk's day to day management of affairs. If they do so regularly, they should not be surprised to receive the Clerk's resignation.

It is important to remember that not every item has to be checked. Sufficient tests should be made to enable the person carrying out the tests to be satisfied that the accounting records are correctly maintained.

Internal Audit

Under Regulation 5 of the Accounts and Audit Regulations 1996, local councils must have an adequate and effective system of internal audit of their accounting records and internal check systems as outlined above. The RFO must make available the relevant financial documents for the purposes of audit and supply the council with relevant information and explanation about such documents.

The internal auditor must be independent and competent – that is he must have experience of local council accounting and/or of auditing. There are several ways of obtaining the services of an internal auditor:

- most county associations of NALC and branches of SLCC will have an established pool of suitably qualified persons;

- the council can employ directly an internal auditor;

- the council can purchase the internal audit service from the principal authority;

- the council can purchase the internal audit service from a local firm of auditors.

It is important to realise that the internal auditor must be independent; the council will have no influence over the work that he considers necessary to undertake. It is, however, possible for the council to ask the internal auditor to undertake additional work at a fee agreed beforehand.

The internal auditor will carry out such tests as are needed to satisfy himself that the internal controls are adequate and are working. The annual report by the internal auditor (part of the Annual Return) contains questions about the following areas:

> A check that proper books of account have been kept
> Checking a sample of payments
> A review of the council's risk assessment
> A check of the precept calculation
> A check of income records
> A review of petty cash records
> A check of salaries
> A check of the asset and investments registers
> A test of bank reconciliations
> A test of the year end financial statements.

As the detail of these checks is not under the control of the council, this book does not need to deal with the actual tasks to be undertaken by the internal auditor. Detailed guidance for the internal auditor is given in *Governance and Accountability in Local Councils in England and Wales – A Practitioners Guide* published by NALC and SLCC.

TABLE 10 – YEAR ENDED 31 MARCH: BUDGET COMPARISON TO 30 SEPTEMBER

	Budget	Actual 30.09	Balance to 31.03
INCOME OR RECEIPTS			
Precept	14,300	14,300	—
Concurrent Functions	11,100	5,550	5,550
Interest on Revenue Balances	1,500	1,100	400
Street Sweeping	1,600	900	700
Open Spaces	1,200	400	800
Cemetery	1,000	450	550
VAT recovered	1,500	800	700
Total Income or Receipts	£32,200	£23,500	£8,700
EXPENDITURE OR PAYMENTS			
General			
Clerk	3,500	1,750	1,750
Insurance and Audit	800	450	350
Room Hire	300	100	200
Office Expenses	950	500	450
Subscriptions	350	300	50
Professional Fees	500	150	350
Sundries/Donations	400	100	300
Election Expenses	900	—	900
s.137	300	200	100
	8,000	3,550	4,450
Open Spaces			
Grass Cutting	3,500	2,800	700
General Maintenance	4,000	3,100	900
Allotments	300	50	250
Common	1,200	400	800
Sundries	100	20	80
	9,100	6,370	2,730

Continued overleaf

51

TABLE 10 (continued)

	Budget	Actual 30.09	Balance to 31.03
Cemetery and Closed Churchyard			
Cemetery Lodge	600	400	200
Cemetery and Lodge Rates and Water	200	110	90
Cemetery Upkeep	6,000	3,500	2,500
Closed Churchyard	1,200	700	500
	8,000	4,710	3,290
Street Sweeping	1,600	900	700
Footway Lighting	1,200	400	800
Village Hall – Contribution	1,000	—	1,000
Contingency	1,500	—	1,500
VAT	1,800	1,000	800
	7,100	2,300	4,800
Total Expenditure or Payments	£32,200	£16,930	£15,270

Chapter 7

EXTERNAL AUDIT

General

The external audit of local councils is now governed by:

- The Audit Commission Act 1998 (the 1998 Act).

- Regulations made thereunder (Accounts and Audit Regulations 1996).

- The Code of Local Government Audit Practice for England and Wales.

The accounts are audited annually by an auditor appointed by the Audit Commission; the auditor may be the District Audit office, an individual or a firm of such individuals who are professional accountants. Auditors are usually appointed on a county by county basis.

Duty to Make Up Accounts for Audit

It is the duty of the Responsible Financial Officer of the council (RFO) to make up the council's accounts as soon as possible after the end of the financial year, and in any event not later than six months after the financial year end. The final accounts must be approved by the council before submission to audit. Where there is a Finance Committee, the final accounts should first be approved by that committee. When presenting the accounts, the RFO should make a brief report pointing out and explaining the salient features, for example instances where expenditure has exceeded the estimates or is greater than the previous year, or where income has not come up to the level expected.

Notice of Audit

The external auditor will set a date when local electors can ask questions about the accounts or object to an item in those accounts.

On receipt of notice of that date, the Clerk must display a notice in a conspicuous place in the parish (e.g. council notice boards) or insert an advertisement in one or more local newspapers for a period of at least 14 days before the date on which the accounts will be made available for public inspection. Having done one or the other, the clerk must immediately send to the auditor either:

(a) a cutting of the advertisement from the newspaper in which it was published, together with a statement of the name and date of publication of the newspaper or newspapers; or

(b) a certificate that the required notices have been displayed in the parish.

It is essential that arrangements are made for publishing the advertisement or putting up the notices immediately the notice is received because the Accounts and Audit Regulations 1996 require that the council's accounts and supporting records and documents must be available for inspection by any member of the public for a period of 15 full working days before the date of the audit, and at least 14 days' notice of the commencement of this period must be given in the public notice or advertisement.

The phrase '15 full working days' used in the Regulations means that the overall period is extended by the number of days (e.g. at weekends which are not working days) when the records are not available. If, for example, the office is only open three days per week, the inspection period of 15 working days will last for 5 weeks.

The Accounts and Audit Regulations 1996 require that the notice of the audit or the advertisement must contain the following information:

(a) the place at which and the hours during which the accounts and other documents will be available for public inspection;

(b) the name and address of the auditor;

(c) the rights available to a local government elector under sections 15 and 16 of the 1998 Act to attend before the auditor either in person or by representative to question him about the accounts and to make objection to those accounts;

(d) the date appointed by the auditor on or after which the rights conferred by sections 15 and 16 may be exercised;

(e) no objection may be made under section 16 of the 1998 Act by or on behalf of a local government elector unless the auditor has previously received written notice of the proposed objection and of the grounds on which it is to be made; and

(f) where an elector sends a notice to an auditor of a proposed objection, he must at the same time send a copy of the notice to the Clerk of the council.

The following is a precedent for a suitable advertisement of public notice of rights of inspection and other public rights which complies with the Regulations. It is a reproduction of Appendix E.1 to *Local Government Audit Law* – 2nd Ed., 1985 by Reginald Jones. It is reproduced with permission of the Audit Commission and has been updated in accordance with current legislation.

Local Council Finance

(NAME OF LOCAL COUNCIL)
AUDIT OF ACCOUNTS
NOTICE OF PUBLIC RIGHTS
Audit Commission Act 1998
Accounts and Audit Regulations 1996, regs. 11, 12, 14 and 15.

Notice is given that from (date) to (date) [a] between (time) and (time) any person interested may inspect, and make copies of, the accounts of the above-named (body) for the year ended 31 March (20**) and all books, deeds, contracts, bills, vouchers and receipts relating thereto. The accounts and other documents will be available for inspection at the offices at which they are normally kept, or otherwise by arrangement; application should be made initially to the Clerk/Finance Officer (address, telephone).

NOTICE is also given that on or after (date) at (time) until the completion of the audit [b] the auditor, at the request of a local government elector for any area to which the accounts relate, will give the elector or his representative an opportunity to question him about the accounts, and that any such elector or his representative may attend before the auditor and make objections as to any matter in respect of which the auditor could take action under section 17 or 18 of the Audit Commission Act 1998 (namely, an unlawful item of account, failure to bring a sum into account, or a loss or deficiency caused by wilful misconduct), or could make a report in the public interest under section 8 of that Act.

Questions and objections may be received at (place of audit) by arrangement with the auditor (name, address, and telephone), to whom requests for this purpose should be addressed. [c] No objection may be made unless the auditor has previously received written notice of the proposed objection and its grounds. A copy of that notice must be sent to the (council) at the address below.

Dated this day of 20**

(Name, office, address)

Notes
[a] With any necessary adaptation to exclude non-working days and to include 15 full working days preceding the date appointed by the auditor under reg. 11/1996. In order to give 14 days' notice, excluding the day of publication and the first day for inspection (reg. 14.1), publication must

be not later than 36 days before the date appointed by the auditor (e.g. 2 Jan. for 7 Feb.); allowance must also be made for public holidays.

[b] The opening date and time is that appointed by the auditor under reg. 11. The regulations do not refer to a terminal date since the rights lapse automatically with the conclusion of the audit. If the audit is expected to be closed soon after the date appointed it is advisable to add a reference to the expected closing date. For small parishes where the audit may be closed on the same day the practical course is to refer only to the appointed date, omitting the words 'or after'.

[c] The regulations do not require the notice to specify the place of attendance. It is generally preferable for notification of questions to be made initially to the auditor's office, arrangements for a meeting, if necessary, being made later. But it may be advisable to include the place of audit in the notice in order to avoid misunderstanding.

Public Inspection of the Accounts

The right of inspection of the accounts and supporting vouchers, etc. prior to audit is for 15 working days, excluding Saturdays and Sundays and any public holidays, before the opening day of the audit. Any 'person interested' has the right to inspect – that is any member of the public and he need not be a local government elector or even a resident in the council's area.

The right to inspection as defined in section 15 of the 1998 Act includes not only the accounts for the year of audit but also all books, deeds, contracts, bills, vouchers and receipts relating thereto; and steps should be taken to ensure that all these are available for inspection at some convenient place. Where a local council has an office, this is the obvious choice; otherwise the accounts and other records could, for example, be made available at the home of the Clerk or the RFO.

Note that Regulation 12.2 states that the council 'shall make the accounts and other documents ... available for public inspection on reasonable notice'. It is designed to prevent individuals turning up without notice at the Clerk's home at an unreasonable time, e.g. 9.00 p.m., which has not been unknown in the past.

The accounts must not be altered after they have been made available for public inspection prior to the audit, except with the express consent of the auditor.

The Annual Return

The Annual Return should be delivered to the auditor with the following sections completed:

1. Section 1 – The Statement of Accounts.

2. Section 2 – Statement of Assurance.

3. Section 4 – Annual Report by Internal Auditor.

Each of the above involve completion of boxes in the Annual Return – a pre-printed form that the external auditor will provide.

The Statement of Accounts

This will be signed by the RFO, stating the basis of preparation (receipts and payments or income and expenditure) and countersigned by the Chairman confirming that the accounts were approved by the council and stating the minute number and date of approval.

The form of accounts is discussed in Chapters 13 and 14.

Statement of Assurance

The council must confirm that it has:

● Approved the accounts which have been prepared in accordance with the Accounts and Audit Regulations 1966.

- Maintained an adequate system of internal control.

- Only done things that it has the legal power to do and has conformed with codes of practice and standards.

- Carried out a risk assessment and dealt appropriately with the issues arising.

- Appointed an internal auditor who is competent and independent.

- Taken appropriate action on matters raised by both the internal and external auditors.

- Given electors the opportunity to inspect and ask questions about the council's business.

- Disclosed everything it should have, including events occurring after the year end.

The council must confirm that the Statement of Assurance has been approved by the council, stating the minute number and date. The Statement will be certified by the Chairman and the Clerk.

Annual Report by the Internal Auditor

The internal auditor makes his report by completing a questionnaire stating whether or not the following tests have been carried out:

- Checks that proper books of account have been kept throughout the year.

- Checks on a sample of payments to ensure that the financial regulations have been adhered to, payments are supported by invoices, etc., expenditure is approved and VAT is accounted for correctly.

- A review of the council's risk assessment, ensuring that adequate arrangements have been made to manage all identified risks.

- Verification that the annual precept has been properly calculated, that the budget has been regularly monitored and that the council's reserves are adequate.

- Checks on income records to ensure that income has been correctly priced, has been received, recorded and promptly banked and VAT is correctly accounted for.

- A review of petty cash records to ensure that they are properly maintained.

- Checks on salaries and wages records, ensuring proper approval and application of PAYE.

- Checks on the accuracy of asset and investment registers.

- Checks on bank reconciliations.

- Checks on the accuracy of year end financial statements.

Explanations on a separate sheet of paper are required in the event of a 'No' answer.

The report will be signed and dated by the internal auditor.

Form of Audit

Note that the banding for audit purposes is *not* the same as for accounts.

Group B – Councils with an income between £100,000 and £500,000

The audit will be a desk-based analytical review, based on a standard checklist produced by the Audit Commission.

A limited number of further tests will be undertaken to check the internal consistency of the figures in the accounts. No detailed testing will be carried out unless the analytical review suggests cause for concern.

Group C – Councils with an income less than £100,000

The audit will be confined to a review of the documents submitted by the council. Further tests would be carried out only if the documents supplied were unsatisfactory.

Additional Audit Work

1. If the Statement of Assurance or the documents provided are unsatisfactory, additional tests will be carried out, the auditor charging for time spent at cost.

2. Councils will be selected on a random basis for a limited number of more detailed enquiries to be carried out. Unless these tests bring to light further areas for concern, there will be no charge by the auditor.

3. A council may request the auditor to undertake additional work at a fee agreed between the parties.

Audit Fee

Fees charged for routine audit are in accordance with a scale laid down by the Audit Commission.

Auditor's Report

The Annual Return includes, in Section 3, the external auditor's Certificate of Opinion – referred to as the Annual Audit Letter in Regulation 16A of the Accounts and Audit Regulations 1996.

The auditor's report will confirm that the audit has been

undertaken in accordance with the Audit Commission's requirements and that no matters have come to the auditor's attention which give cause for concern that the relevant legislative and regulatory requirements have not been met.

When Section 3 of the Annual Return has been completed by the external auditor, the Return will be sent back to the council.

Publication of Accounts

Small councils	Publish Receipts and Payments Account with Annual Audit Letter within nine months of the year end.	Regulation 9(5)
Medium sized councils	Publish Income and Expenditure Account with Annual Audit Letter within nine months of the year end.	Regulation 9(3)&(4)
Large councils	Publish Statement of Accounts with Annual Audit Letter within nine months of the year end.	Regulation 9(1)

Advertise Conclusion of Audit

| All councils | Advertise by notice in a conspicuous place with specified details. | Regulation 16(3) |
| | Notify auditor that this has been complied with. | Regulation 16(4) |

Not later than 14 days after the meeting at which the auditor's report is taken into consideration, the local council, or the Chairman of the parish meeting, must publish (in the same way as the notice of audit is advertised) the Statement of Accounts and Auditor's Report. This can be done by displaying pages 1 to 3 of the Annual Return.

The Rights of Local Government Electors

Any person who appears on the electoral roll for the area of a local council or a parish meeting has the right to attend before the auditor in person or by representative at the time and date appointed by the auditor and to question him about the accounts. If a local government elector is dissatisfied about any matter in the accounts, that is, he suspects or has knowledge of fraud or misconduct in relation to that matter or he considers that an item of expenditure is contrary to law, he has the right to object about it to the auditor. In addition, he has the right to object to the auditor about any matter on which the auditor could make a report in the public interest. An objector must send a written notice to the auditor of his objection and of the grounds on which it is made and at the same time send a copy to the Clerk of the council.

If he is dissatisfied with the auditor's decision on his objection, the local government elector can require the auditor to state his reasons in writing if the objection relates to alleged illegality, loss due to wilful misconduct or failure to bring a sum to account. However, this right does not extend to any matter on which the auditor could make a report in the public interest.

The objector must make the application within six weeks of being notified of the auditor's decision. He then has a right of appeal within 28 days from the day on which he received the auditor's statement of reasons. The right of appeal is to the High Court but an appeal may be made to the County Court if the sum involved is within the financial limits of the jurisdiction of that court in relation to contracts.

As a part of the new approach to auditing, it is proposed that legislation be introduced to revise the rights of electors.

It is suggested that the following changes might be considered:

- primary responsibility for answering questions about the accounts should be with the council;

- introduce a *de minimis* level below which questions and objections will not be considered;

- limiting the use of electors' rights to cases in which a quorum of electors want the issue to be pursued.

Powers and Duties of the Auditor

The auditor's powers and duties are contained in sections 5 and 6 of the 1998 Act. Auditors are required not only to satisfy themselves that the accounts have been properly prepared and comply with the appropriate Regulations (currently the Accounts and Audit Regulations 1996), but also that the body under audit has made proper arrangements for securing economy, efficiency and effectiveness in its use of resources. He has the duty to report on any matter coming to his notice in the course of the audit which he considers is in the public interest and, if he considers it appropriate, can issue his report immediately without waiting to conclude the audit.

The auditor must comply with the Audit Commission's Code of Audit Practice.

The auditor not only has special powers and responsibilities for hearing objections to the accounts but also has certain powers and duties to deal with illegality, failure to account, and losses caused by wilful misconduct. If it appears to the auditor that an item of account is contrary to law, he may apply to the court for a declaration to that effect, except where the item has been sanctioned by the Secretary of State. If it appears to the auditor that:

(a) any person has failed to bring into account any sum which should have been so included and that the failure has not been sanctioned by the Secretary of State; or

(b) that a loss has been incurred or a deficiency caused by the wilful misconduct of any person,

then he must certify that the sum or, as the case may be, the amount of the loss or deficiency is due from that person. (It was decided some years ago in *Re Dickson* (1948) 2 KB 95 that the words 'any person' in this context relate only to members and officers of the authority.)

Any member or officer aggrieved by a decision of an auditor certifying that a sum or amount is due from him has the same right to require the auditor to state his reasons in writing and to appeal to the court as any other person aggrieved by a decision of an auditor (see above under 'The Rights of Local Government Electors').

Where a court finds, on the application of an auditor, that an item of account is contrary to law, the court may order that the members or officers responsible for incurring or authorising the unlawful expenditure shall repay it in whole or in part to the authority, and may order any member, where the unlawful expenditure exceeds £2,000, to be disqualified from being a member of a local authority for a specified period. Where an auditor certifies that a sum in excess of £2,000 is due from a member because of a loss or deficiency due to his wilful misconduct, then that member is disqualified from being a member of a local authority for a fixed period of five years.

Extraordinary Audit

Under section 25 of the 1998 Act, the Audit Commission has the authority to direct the holding of an extraordinary audit of a local council's accounts for any reason which appears proper to it. In particular, the Commission may direct the holding of an extraordinary audit:

- arising out of an application by a local government elector; or

- in response to a request from the authority itself; or

- because of a report made by an auditor regarding irregularities which he has found during the course of the audit.

An extraordinary audit may be held after three clear days' notice has been given in writing to the local council, or Chairman of the parish meeting, in respect of which the audit has been directed to be held. An extraordinary audit need not be advertised unless the Commission directs that it should.

The Audit Commission in its direction for the holding of an extraordinary audit will specify the extent of the audit, that is, the period to be covered by the audit and the accounts or transactions to be examined. All the provisions relating to the annual audit, except the right of public inspection of the accounts and the right to question the auditor, are applied to an extraordinary audit. The right of objection, and the powers and duties of the auditor, are the same as those which apply to an ordinary audit.

The Secretary of State holds a reserve power to require the Commission to direct the holding of an extraordinary audit.

Chapter 8

VALUE ADDED TAX

Introduction

This chapter is divided into five sections, namely:

A. General
B. Local Councils Not Registered for VAT
C. Local Councils Registered for VAT
D. Accounting for VAT
E. Conclusion.

Section C includes sub-sections as follows:

Letting of Sports Facilities
Non-Business Activities
Helping Other Bodies
Exempt Supplies
Miscellaneous Matters.

For those local councils which are not registered for VAT, Sections A, B, D and E are most relevant. In addition, the sub-sections in Section C on Non-business Activities, Helping Other Bodies and the paragraph on default interest and penalties under Miscellaneous Matters may also be of interest to these councils.

For those local councils which are registered for VAT, Sections A, C with sub-sections, D and E are most relevant.

A. General

Value Added Tax (VAT) is a tax on consumer expenditure. The basic UK VAT law is contained in the Value Added Tax

Act 1983, as amended by subsequent Finance Acts and VAT Acts. In addition there are detailed rules in Statutory Instruments in the form of orders made by the Treasury or regulations made by Customs and Excise (C & E). The latter also issue notices and leaflets explaining how they interpret VAT law.

VAT takes two forms – 'output tax' and 'input tax'. Output tax is the VAT charged by a taxable person on the value of the taxable supplies he makes in the course of his business. Input tax is the VAT paid by that person on the goods and services used in the business. In general, input tax can be set against output tax. If the latter exceeds the former, the balance is paid to C & E, if *vice versa*, C & E makes a refund to the taxable person on receiving a properly completed VAT Return.

Local councils have to charge and collect VAT on such of their activities as attract the tax (output tax) and pay VAT (input tax) in accordance with current VAT law on materials, goods and services they use. They are, however, exempt from eventually bearing any VAT they have paid on goods and services in connection with the day to day running of the council. Obviously they are accountable to Customs and Excise for the VAT they collect.

The activities of many smaller local councils are not subject to output VAT because they only participate in 'non-business activities'. Their involvement with VAT will therefore only relate to what they paid to their creditors (input VAT) and its eventual recovery from C & E.

Some of the activities of the larger local councils will inevitably attract output VAT. These are known as 'taxable supplies'. A person or organisation making such supplies is a 'taxable person' and must normally register for VAT with C & E. Because local councils are exempt from bearing any VAT, unlike ordinary businesses, they do not benefit from the annual registration limits. Therefore a local council must register with C & E for VAT purposes if it makes *any* taxable supplies, whatever their value.

This registration requirement can create significant administrative expense where, for example, a local council has not previously made any taxable supplies and it disposes of a second-hand piece of equipment or charges for a photocopy. Where such sales are made by an unregistered local council, discretion may be used by an individual VAT Office in pursuing registration. There is no specific statutory provision for this and it is left to local decision by each VAT Office to ensure that each case is looked at on its merits, following receipt of a written application from any unregistered local council.

B. Local Councils Not Registered for VAT

From the general notes above it should be clear that there will be many smaller local councils which quite correctly do not need to be registered for VAT. All the input VAT they have paid to their creditors is therefore recoverable from C & E.

VAT Notice 749 *Local Authorities and Similar Bodies* explains the refund scheme for both councils which are registered for VAT and those which are not. Copies of Notice 749 can be obtained free of charge from local VAT Offices.

A council which is not registered for VAT should apply in writing for a refund to:

H.M. Customs and Excise
ASD 2C U/B
2nd Floor West, Alexander House
21 Victoria Avenue
Southend-on-Sea, Essex SS99 2QR.

The first application is made by letter, setting out the details. The refund will be made by payable order and a Form VAT 126 will be sent for the next claim. These should normally be made quarterly or half-yearly, unless the amount involved is small, i.e. less than £100, in which case annual submission should be made as soon as possible after the end of the financial year. Details of the individual invoices which go to make up the claim must be listed on the reverse of Form VAT 126 under the column headings printed on the form.

The amount of the claim is normally repaid to a council's bank account within a week of the receipt of the claim at Southend. Finally, do be clear that your council is correctly not registered for VAT. If C & E discover that a council which is not registered should in fact be registered, that council may be liable for penalties and interest.

C. Local Councils Registered for VAT

The business activities of those councils which are registered for VAT involving the supply of goods and/or, more usually, services are either taxable or exempt. For taxable supplies there are now three rates of VAT – zero, 5% for domestic fuel, and standard (currently $17\frac{1}{2}\%$). It is important to realise that 'zero' is a rate of tax. Where supplies are exempt, no VAT is payable. This is a very important point and is discussed more fully later in this chapter under the heading 'Exempt Supplies'.

The activities and supplies of local authorities can be classified into groups. A comprehensive classification is contained in VAT Notice 749A *Local Authorities and Similar Bodies – VAT Status of Activities*. The parts of this notice that are most likely to be of relevance to local councils are as follows:

70

I   Cemeteries and crematoria;

III Entertainment, culture and recreation;

IV Environment and health;

V   Housing and highways;

IX Water;

XI Miscellaneous.

Within each classification individual activities are listed, together with their VAT treatment.

When making a taxable supply, a local council must charge VAT at the appropriate rate. If it fails to do so, it will nevertheless be treated by C & E as having done so and will have to account for and pay the VAT involved. In such circumstances, it is unlikely that the council will be able to recover the VAT from the person to whom it has made the supply because it will have been paid for at the time, especially if that person is not VAT-registered.

Where the appropriate rate is zero, the council does not of course charge VAT, but the difference between a zero-rated supply and an exempt supply must be kept in mind. With a zero-rated supply, it will be possible to offset any input tax the council has paid. See later in this chapter for the section on exempt supplies.

Local councils should therefore obtain a copy of Notice 749A (available free, from local C & E offices) and study the classification in order to ascertain whether or not they are making, or are proposing to make, taxable supplies.

When a local council wishes to be registered for VAT, application should be made to the local VAT Office or to the Regional Advice Centre (telephone numbers and addresses are in the telephone directory under 'Customs and Excise'). After the application has been processed, a

VAT registration number will be allocated and a registration certificate issued. A VAT Return Form VAT 100 will then be sent. These forms are normally returned quarterly but the first one is sometimes for a shorter period. It is essential that the forms run co-terminously with the financial year otherwise unnecessary work is created. Therefore the last VAT 100 in the financial year should be for the quarter ended 31 March; the other quarters will then fall into place automatically. If that is not the case, the quarters should be changed by arrangement with Customs and Excise.

Some guidance on completing Form VAT 100 is included in Section D of this chapter under the heading 'Accounting for VAT'.

Letting of Sports Facilities

There are special rules covering the letting of sports facilities. Normally these are standard-rated supplies. The following are, however, exempt:

(a) a letting or hiring for a continuous period of more than 24 hours where the hirer has exclusive use of the facilities throughout the period;

(b) a series of ten or more lets, whether or not exceeding 24 hours in total, if the following conditions are met:

    (i)   each let is for the same activity in the same place;

    (ii) the interval between lets is not less than one day and not more than 14 days;

    (iii) payment must be for the whole series of the lets and is so evidenced in writing;

    (iv) the lessee/hirer has exclusive use of the facilities; and

(v) the lessee/hirer is a school, a club, an association or an organisation representing affiliated clubs or constituent associations.

VAT leaflet 742/1 *Letting of Facilities for Sport and Physical Recreation* gives detailed guidance on the scope of the legislation. A council making exempt supplies of the kind described in the leaflet may be able to choose to standard-rate them under the 'option to tax' if it is advantageous to that council to do so. More information about that option is given in VAT Notice 742 *Land and Property*.

Non-Business Activities

A non-business activity is either (a) one which is neither actually or potentially in competition with a similar activity in the private sector or (b) free provision of goods and services. A local council may claim a refund of the VAT incurred on non-business activities provided that it:

(a) places the order for the goods or services;

(b) receives the supply;

(c) makes payment from its own funds (but see 'Helping Other Bodies' below for a partial exemption to this proviso).

Helping Other Bodies

As a general rule (VAT Notice 749) a local council cannot use its right to a refund of VAT to benefit other bodies by acting as their agent. It is thus an unlawful evasion of VAT for a council to purchase something on behalf of a village hall committee, reclaim the VAT and obtain reimbursement from the committee (whether before or after the purchase). However, there is an exception to this rule.

A local council may purchase goods or services and donate them to a voluntary body, e.g. a village hall committee, if they are paid for by a grant, e.g. from the District Council, or are paid for with donations from fund-raising or from the management committee. The grant or donation is a non-business activity and is therefore eligible for a refund of VAT. Sufficient records for the purchase must be kept so that the purpose for which it was made can be readily identified.

Exempt Supplies

An exempt supply is a supply of goods or services used in the course of business that is declared by VAT law not to be chargeable to VAT. An exempt supply is distinct from a taxable supply and from a non-business supply (which is not liable to VAT anyway). As indicated above, the vital difference between a taxable and an exempt supply is that no input tax can be recovered on expenditure incurred in relation to an exempt supply.

The major areas where local councils are likely to make exempt supplies are as follows:

(a) letting of land or buildings, e.g. lease of a village hall to trustees, allotment tenancies, lease of sports pitches to football and cricket clubs;

(b) letting of halls or rooms, where there is a licence to occupy land, or a building (or a part thereof, e.g. a room);

(c) long term lets of sport facilities;

(d) a series of lets of sports facilities;

(e) running of a cemetery, though this is likely to cover both taxable and exempt supplies, i.e. partial exemption.

A licence to occupy land is an exempt supply only where the licensee is granted occupation of a clearly defined area to the exclusion of other people not within his control. Thus the hiring out of a hall, or a room, for a purpose on terms which give the hirer exclusive control over the hired area for the duration of a hiring period is an exempt supply. By contrast, granting a right of entry to a sporting or entertainment event does not give exclusive control to the grantee and the supply is therefore taxable.

As indicated above, VAT incurred on purchases for exempt business activities cannot, in principle, be reclaimed. However, it can be reclaimed if the amount of VAT incurred is insignificant, i.e. within the current limits which are:

● not more than £625 a month on average (£7,500 a year); or

● less than 5% of the total VAT incurred on all purchases, including those for non-business activities.

Where there is a large expenditure such as the refurbishment of a hall, a council will certainly exceed the above limits. It may be possible to overcome this problem to some extent by spreading the work over two years and keeping within the limits for at least one of the years.

In order to mitigate the effect of the exempt business supplies trap, a council should attribute the VAT it incurs to the following:

(a) non-business activities;

(b) taxable business activities; and

(c) exempt business activities.

In one instance a local VAT Office agreed, after consultation with its Head Office, that because expenditure at the cemetery covered both taxable and exempt supplies, and as there were no purchases in the financial year attributable entirely to exempt income, all input tax was deductible. In another concerning a community centre, and again, only after consultation with Head Office, a local VAT Office confirmed that any VAT incurred relating to the general running costs of the centre (e.g. repairs to property) is regarded as being attributable to both taxable and exempt supplies. This tax can therefore be excluded when calculating the amount of tax directly attributable to exempt supplies.

Partial exemption will need to be monitored each quarter, by looking at input tax on supplies purchased only for exempt activities as a percentage of the total of the input tax. This percentage should be reviewed at each year end, so that any input tax not claimed, because it exceeded the 5% limit in one quarter, may be deductible if the yearly percentage of input tax attributable to exempt supplies does not exceed 5% of the total input tax for that year. VAT Notice 749 includes an example of a partial exemption calculation at Appendix E.

Miscellaneous Matters

The sale of land by a local council is a standard rate supply. In the case of letting or licensing, the council has an option to charge VAT. In view of the difficulties which exempt business activities often entail, a local council will be well advised to consider exercising this option and charge VAT and thus be able to reclaim input tax in full. If a local council wishes to exercise this option, it must write to its local VAT Office for a letter of authority to do so.

The Finance Act 1985 (sections 14 and 18) introduced new default interest and serious misdeclaration penalty provisions. Local councils therefore need to take particular care that their VAT accounts and returns are correct. Errors in prescribed accounting periods resulting in a net payment becoming due to C & E which are brought to light as a result of a VAT inspection visit will now attract interest and probably a serious misdeclaration penalty as well. Errors in any single VAT accounting period found by a local council, provided they amount to £1,000 or less, can be counted as true tax for that period and adjusted in the following period. They do not have to be notified to C & E, nor do they attract interest. Any errors in excess of £1,000 must be notified to C & E and will attract interest. If in doubt about any VAT matter, you should consult your local VAT Office in writing.

D. Accounting for VAT

A local council should keep its accounting records in such a way as to be able to identify the VAT element in every transaction and should obtain a VAT invoice for all taxable supplies received. Where a local council is registered for VAT, it must provide a VAT invoice showing its VAT registration number when it makes a taxable supply. Where a standard Receipts and Payments Book is in use, the VAT columns on the receipts side and on the payments side should be used to record the VAT.

Where a local council is not registered for VAT, the VAT column on the receipts side will normally merely record the receipt of VAT refunds. The column on the payments side will record the VAT on each taxable supply as the payment is made. The reverse side of Form VAT 126 can then be completed from this column although it will probably be necessary to refer to the individual VAT invoices to obtain the relevant VAT registration numbers.

Where a local council is registered for VAT, the total of the VAT collected (output tax) as shown in the VAT column on the receipts side will be entered in Box 1 of Form VAT 100. The total of the VAT paid (input tax) as shown in the VAT column on the payments side will be entered in Box 4. The difference between the two boxes will be entered in Box 5. If Box 1 is greater than Box 4, then a cheque for the difference will have to be sent to Southend along with the VAT 100. If the reverse is the case, a refund will be due from C & E.

E. Conclusion

The foregoing is a summary of the legal and accounting provisions. Detailed guidance (in clearly written English) is given in C & E VAT notices. Every local council should have a copy of VAT Notice 749 *Local Authorities and Similar Bodies* and VAT Notice 749A *Local Authorities and Similar Bodies - VAT Status of Activities*. Councils which let premises, lease land or contemplate selling land, or make other exempt supplies should also have copies of:

> VAT Notice 742 *Land and Property*
> VAT Notice 706 *Partial Exemption*
> VAT Leaflet 742/1 *Letting of Facilities for Sports and Physical Recreation*
> VAT Notice 708/2 *Construction Industry*.

A useful but not essential publication is VAT Notice 700 *The VAT Guide*, a general guide to the VAT legislation.

All VAT notices are obtainable free of charge from local VAT Offices or from Regional Advice Centres (telephone numbers and addresses are in the telephone directory under 'Customs and Excise').

If you need advice from your local VAT Office, make sure that you get it in writing. VAT Offices have been known to give wrong advice – if that advice is in writing and the VAT Office subsequently changes its earlier ruling, any VAT that has been claimed as input tax cannot be recovered by the VAT Office retrospectively.

Chapter 9

THE PAYROLL

General

Payroll administration is of major importance in every organisation however large or small. Payroll administration usually handles everything the employee receives from the employer for his labour. Over the years this work has become more complicated because of modern legislation and increasing demands, particularly external, for payroll information. This chapter deals only with the subject in broad outline – there are numerous excellent textbooks which deal with it in detail. Although local councils usually employ few staff, many of whom are part-time, some basic knowledge about payroll matters is essential.

Payroll administration work comprises paying staff their remuneration, paying tax and National Insurance deductions to the Inland Revenue collector, calculating sick pay and maternity benefits, sending PAYE returns to the Inland Revenue, and providing statistics and figures for financial accounting purposes.

Other ancillary work includes monitoring annual leave, recording sick leave and attendance, maintaining personnel records and dealing with any routine employment law issues as they arise.

Main Payroll Functions

The main payroll functions are:

(a) calculating gross pay;

(b) calculating all deductions to give an employee's net pay;

(c) processing payslips and updating payroll records;

(d) payment of net pay either in cash, by cheque or some form of bank transfer;

(e) distributing payslips;

(f) payment of deductions to the Inland Revenue, pension fund and trade unions, etc;

(g) keeping all necessary tax, National Insurance and similar records, completing forms as required and making appropriate returns; and

(h) preparing pay statistics and reports.

Nowadays quite small payrolls run economically on a computer. However, where there are only a few employees, it may be more practical to prepare the payslips entirely by hand and to use the Inland Revenue's deduction working sheets P11 to record gross pay and tax and NI deductions, etc.

There are two main and quite distinct steps in preparing an individual's pay. First, the employee's gross pay is calculated. This step depends on how a person's pay is calculated, i.e. by reference to hourly, weekly or monthly rates or scales and whether timesheets are required. In addition, some allowances, e.g. lump sum car allowances, may be included with pay.

Secondly, the tax, National Insurance and pension fund payments are calculated and any other adjustments made to the employee's gross pay. The two steps may be carried out by different means. This has the benefit of acting as a check. For example, gross pay may be calculated manually but net pay by computer.

It is necessary with all payroll systems, manual or

computerised, not to overlook unusual items. Such items comprise pay advances, attachment of earnings orders, repayment of car loans, subscriptions to trade unions and any other similar items. A manual system is operated by using either a bound book or loose-leaf stationery.

The Pay As You Earn (PAYE) system is an effective method of collecting Income Tax and National Insurance contributions. The employer is responsible for collecting the tax and National Insurance contributions from employees every pay period and paying the money over to the Inland Revenue.

When an organisation registers for PAYE, the Inland Revenue will set up a PAYE scheme for the organisation and supply a pack with stationery for recording gross pay, tax, National Insurance, statutory sick pay (SSP) and statutory maternity pay (SMP). However, these forms are more limited than many of the commercially produced systems on the market which are more suitable for a manual system, and they are of course more limited than specially designed computer systems.

At the end of the year, a number of PAYE forms (in particular P14, P35 and P60) have to be prepared for the Inland Revenue. At best this is a lengthy job and to make it less difficult the usual technique of cross-casting and check totals should be used.

Computerisation

A computerised system can either be run in-house or the job can be given to a computer bureau. Now that computers are relatively inexpensive and simple to use there is less need to go to a bureau. In fact it may be almost as much work to prepare the data for a bureau as to process it in-house. The bureau will charge for processing and delivery and then there is the wait for the printed payroll to arrive. It must then be checked and errors corrected via the bureau.

As payroll software can, and should be, bought 'off the shelf', a major consideration is how a package will relate to other parts of the system, i.e. where will the input come from and what will the output be used for? These questions will be determined by cost and how far the payroll system will be integrated into the rest of the accounting system. For input, the main consideration is how much analysis is required of basic pay.

The input data for outside staff usually comes from timesheets and will almost certainly include some analysis. This may mean that the hours worked are analysed over appropriate expense codes as necessary, or (for a simpler analysis) the code may be included on the file containing the employee's personal details. For clerical, administrative and professional staff, such a requirement is less likely, though still possible.

The output will provide the information required for the financial accounts and the final ledger. Output data will usually be used to prepare the cheques or bank transfer documents. In the latter case, it may be desirable for the software to be compatible with that of the bank.

Payment – Cash or Cashless Pay

The essential main objective of any payroll administration is the punctual and accurate payment of employees' wages.

Employees are still sometimes paid in cash, i.e. in banknotes and coins. In recent years, however, most employees, with their agreement, have been paid by cheque or bank transfer. The legal right to be paid in cash was finally abolished by the Wages Act 1986, which gives employers the right to pay employees by cheque or bank transfer if engaged on or after 1 January 1987. If their contract of employment requires it, employees engaged before that date may still demand to be paid in cash.

Payment in cash is to be discouraged for various reasons, for example the security problems involved, the time-consuming nature of cash payment, additional bank charges for notes and coins and the need for control and custody of unclaimed pay packets.

Local councils should therefore make it a condition of service of their staff that pay is cashless, preferably by bank transfer. The bank charges for the latter are less than for payment by cheque.

Cashless Pay

Cashless pay means payment by cheque or by bank transfer.

Cheques are either open or crossed. An open cheque can be cashed on presentation at the branch of the bank on which it is drawn or at any other branch (not necessarily of the same bank) provided the employer has made arrangements with that branch. These cheques may also be drawn on the Girobank or cashed at a stipulated Post Office.

A crossed cheque may only be paid into a bank or equivalent account and is much more secure. Such cheques cannot be drawn on until they have cleared, normally after four working days, but longer in the case of some building society accounts. Because of this, payment should be made at least four working days before the end of the month or the pay period. A crossed cheque can be opened by deleting the crossings and writing over them 'Please pay cash' and duly signing the alteration, unless it is crossed 'Account Payee'.

For bank transfers, specially pre-printed stationery provided by the bank is used. The employer lists on it the name of each employee and the amount to be credited (net pay) to the employee's account by the bank. The employer totals and signs the form, thus authorising the bank to debit that total to his account.

Gross Pay Calculations

Gross pay comprises an employee's basic pay plus any other special payments to which he or she may be entitled.

For the purposes of local councils, basic pay is likely to be calculated by reference to two different factors:

(a) a fixed weekly, monthly, or annual rate, or a pay scale; or

(b) according to the number of hours worked at an agreed hourly rate.

For monthly paid staff, the basic pay for the month is one-twelfth of the annual rate, irrespective of the length of the month.

For weekly paid staff, the pay rate is usually an agreed hourly rate multiplied by the number of hours worked in the week. Where the rate is an annual one, the basic pay is 1/52 of the annual rate.

Any fraction of a penny is always rounded up. If someone has an annual pay of £10,000, the monthly rate works out at £833.3333. This should always be paid as £833.34, even though it makes the annual pay up to £10,000.08.

A lunar month of four weeks can be used instead of a

calendar month. If this system is adopted, the pay is calculated as 1/13 of the annual total. Unless there is a pre-determined agreement to the contrary, the rule is that a week starts on Sunday and a month starts on the first.

Where employees are paid according to the number of hours worked, the hours actually worked (and any other allowances, for example, double time for weekend working) should be multiplied by the hourly rate. Again, any fractions of a penny are rounded up to the nearest whole penny.

Overtime can be unpaid, paid at the standard hourly rate, or paid at a higher rate, for example time and a half. If the council does not specifically state that overtime is to be paid, then any extra hours worked are unpaid. If the council does agree to pay overtime, but does not set a rate, then the basic hourly rate will apply.

Bonuses in the public sector are not as wide-ranging as in the private sector and are rarely, if ever, in kind. They are usually related to:

(a) performance;

(b) status, for example a chargehand allowance; or

(c) are given to all staff in particular grades or specialisms and are related to their basic pay.

Bonuses paid in cash are subject to tax and National Insurance. Bonuses paid in kind are not always subject to National Insurance but are usually subject to tax. As legislation changes frequently, you should check with the local tax office before making tax free payments.

If an advance of pay is made, it will not be subject to tax or National Insurance. It will be deducted from the net pay when the next payslip is made up. Any advance payments are agreed between employer and employee, usually following a request by the employee. When an employee switches from weekly to monthly pay, either because he or she is new or because his or her conditions of service have been changed, an advance of pay is always justified since, without an advance, the employee would have to manage for a month on one week's pay.

Net Pay Calculations

When all deductions have been made from gross pay, the resulting figure is net pay. Deductions may only be made from an employee's pay:

(a) for superannuation or pension deductions in accordance with the scheme to which the employee contributes;

(b) for Income Tax and National Insurance – as required by statute;

(c) for cash shortages incurred by an employee with cash collection duties – as permitted by statute;

(d) in accordance with the terms of a written contract (for example, trade union subscriptions or car loan repayments);

(e) to correct a mistake in a previous payslip;

(f) as required by a court order (for example, attachment of earnings order); and

(g) if an employee has taken part in a strike or other industrial action.

Pension Contributions

The most common pension scheme to which a local council

employee will contribute is the Local Government Pension Scheme. The employee contributes a percentage of his or her gross pay – 6% for officers and 5% for manual workers. The employer's contribution is fixed by the actuary of the fund concerned and is reviewed every three years. To enhance his or her pension, an employee can make additional contributions which, together with the basic contribution, are subject to a maximum – currently 15% of gross pay. The employees' and employer's contributions are payable to the pension fund operated by the County Council in whose area the local council is situated.

An employee can also make additional voluntary contributions (AVCs) to any pension scheme which is approved by the Inland Revenue for Income Tax purposes. Again, the current maximum of 15% applies.

Instead of contributing to the Local Government Pension Scheme, a local council employee can participate in any personal pension scheme approved by the Inland Revenue for Income Tax purposes. Many clerks and other local council employees are not eligible for the Local Government Pension Scheme. In such cases, they should seriously consider a personal pension scheme.

Stakeholder Pensions

Employers with more than five employees must provide access to a Stakeholder Pension Scheme for those employees who are not members of an occupational pension scheme. Arrangements are made with a pensions provider who will deal directly with the employees. Note that employees do not have to join a stakeholder scheme but the scheme must be made available. The employer does not have to contribute.

Income Tax

An employer has a statutory obligation to deduct Income Tax from an employee's earnings if the employee is subject to the Pay As You Earn (PAYE) system. The tax is deducted from gross pay in accordance with each employee's PAYE tax code as notified to the employer by the Inland Revenue.

For Income Tax purposes, gross pay consists of all salaries, wages, commissions, bonuses and other cash payments made by the employer to the employee. It also includes any maternity pay, sick pay or holiday pay and half of any performance-related pay which meets the conditions for tax relief. Allowances for such things as tools, clothing and travel are also taxable as are lump sum allowances (all by adjustment of the employee's tax code), unless the allowance merely reimburses the employee's actual expenses or the employer has a dispensation from the Inland Revenue. The whole of any home to work travel allowance is taxable without any deductions.

Lump sum payments on termination of employment may be taxable. This will be the case if the employee has a contractual right to the sum, and where a termination payment exceeds a certain amount, currently £30,000 (note that only the excess is taxable). Therefore, if the termination payment is less than £30,000, it is not taxable provided that the payment conforms with the tax rules.

To calculate gross pay for tax purposes, certain deductions are allowed from the gross pay as calculated above. These comprise:

(a) pension contributions to the Local Government Pension Scheme plus any contributions to an additional voluntary scheme up to a maximum of 15% of gross salary; and

(b) contributions under a payroll giving scheme.

National Insurance

National Insurance contributions are paid to finance state occupational benefits such as unemployment benefit, state sickness benefits and state pensions. Contributions are assessed on a daily basis instead of on a cumulative basis, as in the case of Income Tax.

Up to a fixed pay threshold, National Insurance is not payable. Once the threshold (which is increased annually in the Budget) is reached, it is payable on the whole amount, not just the excess.

The employer as well as the employee pays National Insurance contributions. There is an upper limit of pay above which the employee pays no more contributions but there is not an upper limit for the employer's contribution. The yield from National Insurance contributions is a major source of revenue to the government and the employer's contribution is in effect a payroll tax.

The contribution is lower if the employee has 'contracted out' and is not contributing to the State Earnings Related Pension Scheme (SERPS), being instead a member of a company or private pension scheme.

National Insurance contributions are not payable if the employee is under 16. Employees stop paying National Insurance on reaching retirement age (65 for both men and women) but the employer continues paying contributions.

National Insurance is paid on the same gross pay figure as Income Tax. However, all of any profit-related pay must be included and no deductions are allowed for pension contributions or payroll giving.

Attachment of Earnings

An employer may be instructed to make deductions from an employee's pay in respect of fines, maintenance payments, etc. under the Attachment of Earnings Act 1971. This also applies to civil debts for which a court judgement has been obtained.

The court will first order the employer to provide details of the employee's earnings so that the amount to be deducted from pay can be decided. Employers are liable to a fine (currently £100) if they fail to do so.

The employer must start to make deductions within seven days of receiving an order. The employer must tell the court within ten days if the employee leaves. The amounts deducted should be paid to the court or other person named in the court order – usually monthly.

Student Loans

Student loans (incurred when the employee was at university) are deductible from earnings. The Inland Revenue will advise you of the amount of the loan to be collected. The weekly/monthly amount to be deducted is calculated by reference to tables provided. Amounts deducted are paid to the Inland Revenue monthly as part of the PAYE payment.

Tax Credits

The employer may have to pay Tax Credits to employees. The amount to be paid will be notified by the Inland Revenue and those amounts paid to employees are deducted from the monthly PAYE payments.

Other Deductions

Any amount authorised in writing by an employee can be deducted from his or her pay. However, an employer can refuse to do so since such arrangements take time and may be inconvenient.

Examples of such deductions include:

(a) repayment of a car loan;

(b) rent of tied accommodation.

Deductions are also made in respect of advance payments and errors outstanding from previous payslips.

Payroll Errors

If an employee is overpaid in error, he or she should be notified immediately. Adjustment will usually be made in the next payslip. However, if an overpayment is large it should be recovered by instalments.

In the case of underpayment, the sum should be offered to the employee immediately, possibly by means of an additional payslip. All corrections should be clearly indicated on the next payslip.

Alterations to Tax and National Insurance

Errors in tax or National Insurance, or in gross pay which affect tax or National Insurance are corrected in the next payslip and the tax and National Insurance records are adjusted at the same time.

It is a statutory requirement that when alterations are made to tax or National Insurance records, both the original and the corrected figures must be legible.

If it is not possible to deduct the full amount of tax or National Insurance, for example because the employee has left, the Inland Revenue and/or Contributions Agency must be informed. They may recover it from the employee by direct assessment but, if they are unable to recover the sum involved from the employee, they will attempt to recover it from the employer, especially if that employer is a public body. There have been cases where local council Clerks have failed to deduct PAYE from their own pay, or have failed to declare to the Inspector of Taxes the amount they have received, and the facts have not come to light until after the Clerk has left the particular local council's employ. The Inland Revenue has then recovered the tax involved from the local council concerned; in some instances quite large sums have been involved.

Remember that the Clerk's salary, however low, is always subject to PAYE and National Insurance deductions. The only exception to this is where the Inland Revenue has notified the council in writing that the Clerk may be paid gross.

Dealing with Inland Revenue and the Contributions Agency

These departments perform an administrative function and are only concerned to ensure that everyone pays what they are statutorily required to pay. Their employees are usually very helpful if you have any queries or problems.

Inland Revenue

Since the computerisation of the department in 1988, which included PAYE, its running has been streamlined and queries are now dealt with more easily and quickly. Errors do still occur, however, as a computer will only print out what is fed into it.

Answer any query from the Inland Revenue promptly. This can often be done over the telephone but more complex queries should be answered in writing and a copy kept. Staff in the PAYE sections of Inspector of Taxes offices are always very helpful in answering queries. The Collector and Inspector are in two different departments, since it is a commonsense accounting requirement that assessment is kept separate from collection. Notifying one of them does not constitute notification to the other. If necessary, letters to one should be copied to the other.

It can often be useful to meet a tax officer if a matter proves difficult to resolve. A meeting will often resolve what correspondence cannot, and more quickly and amicably as well.

Tax Investigations

Every so often, the Inland Revenue will conduct an audit of an employer's payroll records. The employer is formally notified that an audit will take place. The audit may be simply a routine one or an error may have been discovered. Alternatively, the employer may have made a voluntary disclosure or information may have been received from another source. The auditor will check the records for tax, National Insurance, statutory sick pay and statutory maternity pay. Employers who use agencies, or who have part-time employees, are more likely to be investigated as tax evasion is more prevalent in such cases.

If agreement cannot be reached with the auditor, then the matter is passed to the Inspector. A hearing can be obtained before the General or Special Commissioners if the employer believes that the Inspector has acted unreasonably.

If a letter is received stating that 'the Inspector has reason to believe the council's tax records are not correct in all respects' (or similar), it means that a back duty investigation has been started and it is important to get specialist advice.

The council may be liable to penalties in the event that irregularities are discovered, even if it is an employee's tax that is owed. The penalties may be lower if the council can show that the irregularity was accidental and if it co-operates with the investigation and takes appropriate steps to avoid the same thing happening again.

VAT inspectors also have rights of access to a council's records but it is most unlikely that they would inspect payroll records because pay is not subject to VAT, unless contract staff are employed.

Contributions Agency

Problems with the National Insurance contributions usually concern missing National Insurance numbers, or claims for pensions or social security benefits by present or former employees. It is important to help to match contributions to National Insurance numbers, otherwise staff will be making contributions without building up the full benefit to which they are entitled.

The Contributions Agency is a department of the Inland Revenue and will also carry out an audit of an employer's payroll records from time to time.

Payslip Guide

It may be useful to Clerks, etc., and to employees, to have a basic guide explaining the layout of a payslip, as follows:

The contents of a payslip

1. *Basic pay* is the amount earned at the normal rate of pay in a pay period.

94

2. *Gross pay* is the total amount earned before any deductions are made. It includes not only basic pay but any other payments earned such as overtime and on-call duties or additional responsibilities allowances.

3. *Pension deductions.* Where an employee is having contributions to the Local Government Pension Scheme deducted from his or her pay, or is making AVCs to an individual pension plan by deduction from pay, these deductions are not taxable. To achieve this they are excluded from the 'gross pay for taxable purposes' (below), by deducting them from the 'gross pay' amount (above).

4. *Gross pay to date for tax purposes* shows the amount earned so far in the tax year which is taxable.

5. *National Insurance number.* Everyone has a different National Insurance number. This ensures that their contributions are correctly credited so that they get their full state pension when they retire and that they can claim the full amount of any social security benefits during their working life.

6. *National Insurance code letter* (a single letter) indicates how much National Insurance should be deducted. If an employee is contracted out of the state pension scheme, the letter is usually D. If the employee is still in the state scheme, the letter is usually A and, for someone 65 or over and still working, the letter is C.

7. *The tax code* indicates how much an employee can earn each week or month before tax is payable. Most tax codes consist of a number followed by a letter. The higher the number is, the less tax is payable. The letter indicates 'tax status'.

The letter is most commonly L for a single person but for a married man or a single parent it is usually H. If a person is single and over 65, it should be P. If the code is BR or OT, this means that there is no tax free allowance and tax is payable on all earnings, probably because the tax allowance is given elsewhere. If an individual believes their tax code is wrong, he or she should take the matter up with the tax office concerned. If he or she is still not satisfied, a right of appeal exists.

Code numbers are notified to the employer by the Inland Revenue.

8. *Free pay* is the amount which can be earned at any time in a given tax year (6 April to 5 April) before tax is payable. The tax code determines how this figure is calculated.

9. *Taxable pay to date* is the gross pay to date less the free pay to date.

10. *Tax to date* is the amount of tax paid so far in any tax year. It is calculated by reference to the tax tables.

11. *Tax due* is the 'tax to date' figure less the cumulative tax paid in previous periods.

12. *National Insurance* is in effect a second Income Tax imposed on employers as well as employees to pay for unemployment benefit and the state pension, etc. If an employee is not 'contracted out', the contribution is helping to fund his or her pension under the SERPS scheme. If an employee is 'contracted out', it means that he or she is in a company or private pension scheme and less National Insurance is paid.

13. *Other deductions and additions*. The reason for other deductions from an employee's pay must be shown on the payslip. The law is quite clear as to what can be deducted. Thus, the only deductions which can be made

are those which an employee authorises (in writing) or those which the law or a court requires an employer to make. Additions to pay, such as Tax Credits, should be shown as separate items.

14. *Net pay* is the amount which the employee actually receives. It is the last item on the payslip and is widely known as 'take-home pay'.

Payroll Accounts

Wages and salaries must be paid on each weekly or monthly pay-day and cannot wait until a cheque is drawn at the monthly meeting of the council. It is therefore essential where the council employs several staff that the Clerk or RFO is provided with funds in a separate bank account out of which to pay the staff and the Inland Revenue, etc.

A payroll account may be operated on an imprest basis or by means of lump sum advances. Under the imprest method, the Clerk or RFO should be advanced a sum of money sufficient to meet the total amount of the net pay, Income Tax and National Insurance likely to become due between one council meeting and the next, plus a margin for safety. At each council meeting thereafter, the separate bank account should be reimbursed for the net pay, etc. actually paid since the previous meeting, thus restoring the balance to its original amount ready to meet the ensuing period's pay, etc.

Under the lump sum method, the amount transferred should be sufficient to meet the total amount of net pay, etc. likely to be needed before the next council meeting after taking into account the amount already in the bank account. Cheques drawn on a payroll bank account need only have one signature as obviously the funds in the account at any one time will be limited.

Chapter 10

CAPITAL ACCOUNTING

Capital Expenditure

Capital expenditure is expenditure on the acquisition, or construction, of an asset which will last for some years. It has practical significance because local councils are only empowered to borrow with the consent of the Secretary of State given under the provisions of Part IV of the Local Government and Housing Act 1989 for this class of expenditure. Such consents take the form of 'credit approvals' which will authorise borrowing for an approved project. Thus, a local council having the necessary credit approval may embark on a scheme involving a heavy outlay without crippling their Council Tax payers by meeting the cost out of a loan and spreading the repayment of the loan over a period of years.

In some cases, capital expenditure produces assets which may be resaleable. The purchase of land and expenditure on the acquisition or construction of buildings falls within this category. In other cases, capital expenditure may produce something which, although of lasting worth to a local council, is not resaleable. Expenditure on the construction of a new tennis court, or the provision of children's playground equipment and safety surface in a recreation ground are examples of this class of capital expenditure which is usually referred to as a 'community asset', to distinguish it from capital expenditure on the acquisition of a capital asset which is resaleable if the local council wishes.

Powers are available for the local council to incur capital expenditure for the purpose of any of their functions.

Section 124 of the Local Government Act 1972 empowers local councils to acquire by agreement any land (and this, of course, includes any building on the land) whether it is situated inside or outside the parish for the purposes of any of their statutory functions or for the benefit, improvement or development of their area. A local council may buy or construct and furnish and equip buildings:

● for use as offices, workshops, etc. under section 111 of the 1972 Act; or

● for use for public meetings and assemblies under section 133 of the same Act; or

● for use as community centres and for a wide range of recreational and sporting purposes under section 19 of the Local Government (Miscellaneous Provisions) Act 1976.

Treatment of Capital Expenditure in the Accounts

Any capital expenditure should be entered in a separate analysis column headed 'Capital Expenditure' in the Cash Book because it is an important single head of expenditure in its own right and should thus receive due prominence.

Accounting Adjustments on the Sale of Land

Subject to certain restrictions (see sections 127 and 131 of the Local Government Act 1972), a local council may sell land which is no longer required. Except with the consent of the Secretary of State, it must be sold for the best consideration that can reasonably be obtained.

In the council's Cash Book, the amount received from the sale of the land should be recorded in a separate column on the receipts side of the account headed 'Sale of Assets'. Segregation of moneys received from the disposal of assets is necessary because there are statutory restrictions on the use which may be made of such capital receipts.

Application of Money Received from the Sale of Land

Capital money received on a disposal of land must be applied towards the discharge of debt or otherwise for a purpose for which capital money may properly be applied. The Secretary of State has given a general consent to this application in DoE Circular 5/87 and Welsh Office Circular 14/87 under powers conferred on him by section 153(2) of the Local Government Act 1972.

Before land acquired for allotments can be sold or otherwise disposed of, the consent of the Secretary of State is required (section 32(1) of the Allotments Act 1908, as amended by section 8 of the Allotments Act 1925 and sections 23 and 26 of the Town and Country Planning Act 1959). Capital receipts from the sale of allotment land must be applied in redemption of allotment debt or in the acquisition, adaptation or improvement of land for allotments. Any surplus remaining can be applied for any purpose for which capital money may be applied (section 32(2) of the Allotments Act 1908 as amended by section 1(5) and Schedule 5 of the Local Government Planning and Land Act 1980). Areas of 250 square yards or less may be appropriated for another purpose (section 8 of the Allotments Act 1925, as amended by section 23 of the Town and Country Planning Act 1959 and section 126 of the Local Government Act 1972); greater areas may be appropriated only with the consent of the Secretary of State.

In the Annual Return, the value of fixed assets at 31 March each year is entered at item 9 of Section 1.

Assets Register

Local councils are required to keep a register to record all their assets. These records take various forms. Some are bound and last for several years, while others are more simple and can be kept on a word processor and updated as required. The register should show at least the following:

● date of purchase;
● description of the asset;
● location of the asset;
● cost and current value of the asset.

An example of this type of simple record is as follows:

TABLE 11 – ABC PARISH COUNCIL ASSET REGISTER

i) **Land**
Land at the Recreation Ground .... Gifted by Mr .... to the Parish Council on 31 December 1929 for use as recreation ground for the children of the parish.

	NIL
Land known as .... purchased in 1981.	28,000
	28,000

ii) **Machinery**

Shane Centurion 75 Tractor Serial No. 6215 Reg. No. .... purchased 27 October 1992 with a Grant from RT Borough Council.	3,300
Grass Harrow purchased 27 October 1992 with a Grant from RT Borough Council.	600
Mower purchased 29 April 1988.	1,160
	5,060

iii) **Playground Equipment**

Purchased 30 December 1991 with a Grant of £8,700 from RT Borough Council.	10,660
Purchased November 2000 with a Grant from RT Borough Council.	3,942
Purchased December 2001 with a Grant from RT Borough Council.	1,625
	16,227

Assets should be valued at 'current book value' which should represent the open market value or, in the case of buildings, the cost of reconstruction. Insured values may be used but adjustment must be made for the reduced value of assets such as vehicles and machinery which decline in value throughout their lives.

Chapter 11

BORROWING

General

A local council may borrow money for any of its statutory functions provided it obtains prior consent to the borrowing. The arrangements are set out in DoE Circular 199/90 *Local Authority Capital Finance* dated 2 August 1990, pending the issue of Regulations under section 39 of the Local Government and Housing Act 1989. Supplementary credit approvals are now issued to enable local councils to borrow to finance a particular project.

Local councils obtain credit approval application forms from the County Associations; after completion, the forms are returned to the County Association. If approved at local level, they are forwarded to the National Association of Local Councils in London and then to the DTLR for an allocation from the national financial pool set up for that purpose in each financial year. It should be noted that a credit approval lapses if it is not exercised by borrowing by the date stated in the approval.

The council must repay or amortise any loan in full at or before the end of the period of years sanctioned for the borrowing. The credit approval sets out this period. Loans must be repaid either by half-yearly or yearly instalments or by setting aside a sum of money each year in a special fund (known as a Sinking Fund) so that at the end of the loan period enough money has accumulated in the fund to repay the loan. In the latter case, interest is paid regularly during the period of the loan. These are known as maturity loans.

A loan which, under the loan agreement, has to be repaid

to the lender by equal half-yearly or yearly instalments (including interest over the loan period) is known as an annuity loan. With each instalment, the lender is paid interest on the balance of the loan outstanding since the previous instalment was paid. Therefore, as the loan is repaid, the amount of interest in each instalment decreases and there is an increase by the same amount in the principal repaid.

Occasionally, loans are raised where the principal is repaid in equal half-yearly or yearly instalments but as a result the interest payments are high in the early years. These are called 'instalment' loans.

Where a capital project is financed by raising a separate 'annuity' loan, it is known as an 'ear-marked' loan. The charge to be made each year to the Revenue Account will be the total (capital and interest) payments made during the year to the lender.

Annuity and maturity loans are available from the Public Works Loan Board and also from District Councils and County Councils; many banks and insurance companies are also prepared to grant such loans. Instalment loans may also be available from some of these sources. Local councils who dispose of assets while loans are still outstanding do not have to repay the loans prematurely if this would be disadvantageous to the local council.

Recording the Receipt and Spending of a Loan

Since loan money may only be spent on the specific purpose for which the loan was authorised, it follows that the receipt and the spending of money raised by way of a loan must be separately recorded in the accounts to ensure that this requirement is met.

Where the accounts are kept on a receipts and payments basis, a separate sub-column should be set aside on the receipts side of the council's Cash Book to record the receipt of loans. Similarly, a special column should be included on the payments side for payments out of borrowed moneys.

The total of loans outstanding at 31 March is shown at item 10 of Section 1 of the Annual Return.

Ways of Providing for the Repayment of a Loan

Once a loan has been raised, a local council must start within the first 12 months to make provision for its redemption, and the loan must be fully redeemed by the end of the period approved by the Secretary of State (paragraph 7, Schedule 13 to the Local Government Act 1972).

As stated earlier in this chapter, repayment of a loan may be effected by any one of the following three methods, or by a combination of them:

    A. Annuity;

    B. Maturity;

    C. Instalment.

A. Annuity Method

Under the annuity method, equal payments are made to the lender each half-year or year and these constant payments include both an element of principal and an element in respect of the interest due on the reducing balance of the principal.

The amount of the fixed sum required each half-year or year to repay a loan on the annuity basis depends on the

TABLE 12 – ANNUITY PAYMENTS

Table of the half-yearly annuity payments required to repay a loan of £100 at stated rates of interest within given periods

Rate of interest p.a.	5 years	*Period in which the loan is to be repaid* 10 years	15 years	20 years	25 years
	£ p	£ p	£ p	£ p	£ p
5%	11.43	6.42	4.78	3.98	3.53
6%	11.72	6.72	5.10	4.33	3.89
7%	12.02	7.04	5.44	4.68	4.26
8%	12.33	7.36	5.78	5.05	4.66
9%	12.64	7.69	6.14	5.43	5.06
10%	12.95	8.02	6.51	5.83	5.48
11%	13.26	8.36	6.88	6.23	5.91
12%	13.59	8.72	7.27	6.65	6.34
13%	13.91	9.08	7.66	7.07	6.79
14%	14.24	9.44	8.06	7.50	7.25
15%	14.57	9.81	8.47	7.94	7.71
16%	14.90	10.19	8.88	8.39	8.17
17%	15.24	10.57	9.31	8.84	8.65
18%	15.58	10.95	9.73	9.30	9.12
19%	15.93	11.35	10.17	9.76	9.60
20%	16.28	11.75	10.61	10.23	10.09

amount of the loan, the rate of interest and the period over which the loan is to be repaid. The lender will normally supply a schedule giving the breakdown of each repayment.

The most common method of borrowing by mortgage employed by local authorities is by means of loans repayable by half-yearly annuities. The table opposite sets out the half-yearly annuity for the repayment of a loan of £100 at 1% intervals from 5% to 20% per annum and for selected periods from 5 years to 25 years. The table will enable calculations to be made sufficiently accurately for the purpose of estimating the annual cost of repaying a proposed loan on the half-yearly annuity basis.

Example

To calculate the amount to be paid each half-year in respect of £2,500 borrowed at an interest rate of 14% per annum for 20 years, read across the line against 14% and take the figure under the vertical column headed '20 years'. This gives the half-yearly annuity for a loan of £100, i.e. £7.50. So, for a loan of £2,500, the half-yearly annuity will be 25 x £7.50 = £187.50. The full annual cost of repaying this loan will, of course, amount to twice the half-yearly annuity payment, i.e. 2 x £187.50 = £375.

B. Maturity Method

Loans may be borrowed which, whilst requiring the payment of interest yearly or half-yearly, provide that the amount borrowed is to be repaid to the lender at the end of the loan period, e.g. in 5, 10 or 20 years. These are known as maturity loans.

Although repayment to the lender is not due until the expiry of the loan period, the council must set aside a sum of money each year in a special fund, called a Sinking Fund, so that by the date the loan is due for repayment sufficient funds have been set aside in the Sinking Fund to repay the loan.

Interest on the full amount of the loan borrowed will be paid to the lender until the loan is repaid to him, usually half-yearly or yearly.

The annual contributions to the Sinking Fund and the interest paid each year to the lender must be charged to the Income and Expenditure Account.

The amounts transferred to the Sinking Fund should be fixed so that at the end of the period there is enough money in the fund to repay the loan in full. For example, in the case of a loan of £1,000 repayable at the end of 20 years, the annual contribution to a non-accumulating Sinking Fund will be £1,000 ÷ 20 = £50.

C. Instalment Method

The amount of the loan is divided by the number of half years or years in the period over which the loan is to be repaid and this amount is repaid to the lender each half year or year together with interest on the balance of the loan outstanding since the repayment of the previous instalment.

In the early years, the combined payment of principal and interest will be heavy because of the large amounts of interest due. As the principal is paid off, the interest charge will fall correspondingly and the combined amount of principal and interest will reduce progressively throughout the period of the loan.

Borrowing by Bank Overdraft or Other Short-Term Means

Local councils are authorised by paragraph 10, Schedule 13 to the Local Government Act 1972 to borrow temporarily for short periods by way of bank overdraft or other short-term means from any institution authorised under the Banking Act 1987. The specific consent of the Secretary of State is therefore not required for this type of borrowing. This borrowing power can only be used as a temporary expedient pending the receipt of revenues due or the raising of a permanent loan. There are time limits for both of these borrowings.

If capital expenditure credit approval has been obtained, a council may borrow on overdraft pending receipt of the loan finance, provided that the loan money is receivable not more than 12 months after the end of the accounting year.

Interest charged by the bank on an overdraft should be charged to the Receipts and Payments Account or Income and Expenditure Account under the heading 'Loan Interest and Loan Repayments'.

Chapter 12

INSURANCE

Introduction

Even the smallest local council needs to consider whether it has any interests which ought to be protected by some form of insurance. The general headings listed below comprise the interests which a council should consider in deciding what insurance cover it needs. It should be remembered, however, that cover must be kept under regular review for it to be up to date and for it to meet new insurance needs as they emerge.

Liabilities – third party
– employer's liability

Property – all risks
– fire and perils
– theft
– impact damage

Fidelity Guarantee

Money

Personal Accident

Libel and Slander

Motor Vehicles.

There follows some brief notes on each of these headings.

Third Party Liability

This insurance covers the legal liability of the council and its employees for claims:

(a) resulting from accidental bodily injury or illness of members of the public; and accidental loss of or damage

110

to property arising in connection with the activities of the council; and

(b) in respect of loss or damage (other than in (a) above) resulting from any negligent act or accidental error or omission committed by employees in carrying out their council duties.

The importance of adequate insurance against third party risks cannot be over-emphasised. If a council owns property, for example children's play equipment or a bus shelter, cover is essential. Insurance cover may also be necessary in other cases, for example where functions are organised by the council. The National Association of Local Councils recommends minimum cover against third-party risks. This figure is published by the Association and is revised from time to time.

Employer's Liability

As employers, parish councils and parish meetings are required by law to insure employees who are employed under a contract of service, written or otherwise, against liability for bodily injury or disease arising out of and in the course of their employment. The insurer will issue certificates of insurance for display and inspection.

Property – All Risks

This covers loss or damage by any cause, subject to certain exclusions such as wear and tear, of such items as office machinery, pictures and trophies.

Property – Fire and Perils

Buildings and their contents should be insured against damage or destruction by fire, lightning, explosion, storm or tempest, flood, bursting or overflowing water tanks, apparatus or pipes, impact, aircraft, riot, civil commotion, strikes, labour disturbances, malicious persons, earthquake and accidental breakage of fixed glass and sanitary ware.

Property – Theft

Property owned by the council, or for which it is responsible, should be insured against theft accompanied by forcible entry to, or exit from, premises or theft accompanied by personal violence, or threat thereof, to council employees.

Property – Impact Damage

This covers accidental damage by impact of any vehicle or animal to footway lighting, bus shelters and street furniture. It may also be appropriate to insure bus shelters under 'Fire and Perils' above.

Fidelity Guarantee

This insurance provides cover against the loss of money or other property belonging to the council through fraud or dishonesty on the part of employees.

Money

This covers money, including cheques, postal orders, stamps, etc. against loss or damage by any cause whilst in certain locations only. It does not cover employees' fraud or dishonesty (which is covered by the fidelity guarantee above), errors in accountancy, or errors in paying out or collecting money. The locations will usually be:

(a) in council offices in the custody of employees or in transit, i.e. to or from the bank or an outstation;

(b) in a safe in council offices overnight; or

(c) in an employee's private residence.

Where cash is kept in a locked drawer or cash box, cover is normally provided but a limit is imposed (usually £250).

Personal Accident

Members, employees and volunteers assisting in the discharge of council functions should be insured against accidents whilst engaged on council business.

Libel and Slander

This type of insurance covers the legal liability of the council, its members and employees for libels in council publications arising in the conduct of council business, for example letters; and for slanders uttered by members or employees in the course of official business and procedures.

Motor Vehicles

Comprehensive cover must be provided for all council-owned vehicles (including tractors) in the normal way. Cover can also be obtained against the contingent legal liability of the council for third party claims arising from the use by members or employees of their own private cars on council business.

General

Some insurance companies offer a 'combined' policy providing all the types of cover required by local councils. Such policies usually cost less than separate policies for each type of insurance. Local councils should seek competitive quotations for their insurance cover from time to time to ensure that they are obtaining the best deal available.

One insurance company that should always be included on the tender list is Municipal Mutual Insurance Ltd. This company was founded at the beginning of the 20th century to form a mutual fund to meet the insurance needs of local government. It has a particular expertise in local government insurance and deals directly with the policy holders, thus avoiding the cost of commissions to intermediaries. Therefore, at least in theory, its premiums should be hard to beat and should always be used as a benchmark for comparison with those quoted by other companies.

Chapter 13

FINANCIAL STATEMENTS – GROUP C COUNCILS WITH INCOME OR EXPENDITURE BELOW £50,000

Local councils are required to prepare annual financial statements in accordance with section 7(3) and (4) of the Accounts and Audit Regulations 1996 (AAR). These are summarised in Section 1 of the Annual Return. All councils should, however, review their budget figures compared with the actual figures for the year ended 31 March.

Many councils will want to give their electors more information than is shown in the Annual Return and may publish their detailed budget statement, perhaps with additional explanatory notes. Larger councils may wish to publish a more formal Profit and Loss Account and Balance Sheet, as were required before the year 2001/02 – this will be dealt with in Chapter 14.

Councils with an income or expenditure below £50,000 are required to prepare a Receipts and Payments Account, which will also include comparative figures, i.e. figures for last year.

Using the example in Table 4 set out in Chapter 3, the final figures for the year are as shown overleaf.

In most cases this format will be adequate to enable the council to answer 'Yes' to question 1 in Section 2 – the Statement of Assurance in the Annual Return.

115

TABLE 13 – RECEIPTS AND PAYMENTS ACCOUNT

	Actual Previous Year	Budget Current Year	Actual Current Year	Budget Next Year
Expenditure	£	£	£	£
1. Administration	4,078	5,500	5,325	5,200
2. Planning	500	500	602	600
3. Sports Field	3,365	1,500	1,476	1,700
4. Play Scheme	1,701	2,000	2,058	2,200
5. Street Sweeping	1,140	1,300	1,371	1,400
6. Litter Bins	—	300	305	400
7. Aid to Village Hall	—	—	450	500
8. Footpaths & Signs	139	300	317	300
9. Grants	—	—	—	—
10. Section 137	—	—	—	—
11. Room Hire for Meetings	225	240	309	350
12. Neighbourhood Watch	75	100	100	100
13. Publicity	375	300	324	300
14. Jubilee Celebrations	—	300	338	—
15. Children's Play Areas	—	—	—	1,500
Gross Expenditure	11,598	12,340	12,975	14,550
Income	£	£	£	£
1. Administration	—	—	—	—
2. Sports Field	52	50	186	400
3. Play Scheme	1,708	1,800	1,843	2,000
4. Street Sweeping	1,157	900	1,146	1,200
5. Concurrent Functions Grant	6,666	3,500	4,193	3,220
6. Bank Interest	64	70	72	60
7. Miscellaneous	490	—	—	—
8. Precept	2,000	6,000	6,000	6,000
Gross Income	12,137	12,320	13,440	12,880
Surplus/(Deficit)	539	(20)	465	(1,670)

From these figures, Section 1 of the Annual Return can be prepared as follows:

1	Balances brought forward	4,054
2	Annual precept	6,000
3	Total other receipts	7,440
4	Staff costs	(4,200)
5	Loan interest/capital repayments	(Nil)
6	Total other payments	(10,775)
7	Balances carried forward	4,519
8	Total cash and investments	4,519
9	Total fixed assets	5,250
10	Total borrowings	Nil

These figures are obtained from:

1. The opening balance in the Cash Book.

2. Item 8 under Income in Table 13 above.

3. Items 1 to 7 in Table 13 above.

4. The total of the staff costs in the Cash Book.

5. The total of any loan interest and capital payments in the Cash Book.

6. The total expenditure, less lines 4 and 5.

7. The balance carried forward in the Cash Book. Note that this figure is also the sum of lines 1 to 3 less the sum of lines 4 to 6.

8. This will be the same figure as in line 7.

9. This will be the total of the current value of assets recorded in the fixed assets register.

10. The total capital value of all borrowings, e.g. PWLB and bank overdrafts.

The Annual Return should be accompanied by an explanation of any significant variations from the previous year and a copy of the bank reconciliation at 31 March.

Chapter 14

FINANCIAL STATEMENTS – GROUP B COUNCILS WITH INCOME OR EXPENDITURE BETWEEN £50,001 AND £500,000

Councils with income or expenditure which is more than £50,000 but less than £500,000 prepare their financial statements on an 'income and expenditure' basis. The Accounts and Audit Regulations 1996 require that an Income and Expenditure Account and a Balance Sheet are required. It is anticipated that the requirement to prepare a Balance Sheet will be removed during 2002/03.

Whilst councils should prepare a final budget comparison for management purposes, many will also wish to prepare a more detailed Income and Expenditure Account. The absolute minimum information is included in Section 1 of the Annual Return, but this alone will not allow the council to answer 'Yes' to question 1 in the Statement of Assurance.

The principles behind income and expenditure accounting are dealt with in detail in Chapter 5 but remember that the adjustments to be made cover:

1. Income due that has not been received.

2. Income that has been received but which relates to the following year.

3. Expenditure that has not been included.

4. Expenditure that has been incurred but which relates to the following year.

5. Stock.

If a double entry book-keeping system is in use, items 1 and 3 should have been dealt with. In all cases, remember to reverse adjustments made at the previous year end.

Taking the example budget in Table 1 set out in Chapter 3, the figures in the 'Actual Current Year' column will need to be adjusted; in practice the adjustments should be made in the detailed subsidiary budgets and carried over to the summary budget. For the purposes of this example, the adjustments will be made in the summary budget, using only the headings required for Section 1 of the Annual Return. The budget must firstly be re-arranged using the headings required for the Annual Return and then adjusted for items 1 to 5 above.

To re-arrange into the Annual Return headings each individual committee budget needs to be examined and the relevant figures extracted. The result would be:

TABLE 14 – ADJUSTED BUDGET

	Planning Committee	Open Spaces Committee	Finance Committee	Total
Income	4,250	44,271	4,592	53,113
Expenditure				
Staff costs	—	124,286	42,700	166,986
Loan interest/capital repayments	—	6,824	9,570	16,394
Other costs	15,135	42,710	50,650	108,495
	15,135	173,820	102,920	291,875
Net expenditure	10,885	129,549	98,328	238,762
Precept				240,000
Surplus for the year				£1,238

The following adjustments have not been made in the above figures and need to be dealt with now:

		Last Year	This Year
1.	Income due from Cofffin & Co – burial fees	650	300
2.	Income received in advance – Community Centre booking fees April/May	250	360
3.	Expenditure not included (creditors) – Repairs to Community Centre	450	570
4.	Expenditure in advance – Grant made last year to Sports Club to cover 3 years	400	200
5.	Stock at the Community Centre	230	380

These adjustments can now be applied to the figures in Table 14:

	Note (above)	Receipts and Payments	Previous Year Adjustments	This Year Adjustments	Income and Expenditure
Balances Brought Forward		44,289	580		44,869
Precept		240,000			240,000
Other Income	1	53,113	(650)	800	
	2		250	(360)	53,153
Staff Costs		(166,986)			(166,986)
Loan Interest/Capital Repayments		(16,394)			(16,394)
Total Other Payments	3	(108,495)	450	(570)	(108,665)
	4		(400)	200	
	5		(230)	380	
Balances Carried Forward		45,527		450	45,977

Comments:

The balances brought forward and carried forward in the Receipts and Payments column are the cash balances from the Cash Book.

121

The adjustment against Balances Brought Forward is the amount required to make the Previous Year column total zero. The adjustment against Balances Carried Forward is the net of all adjustments in the This Year column.

Both the Receipts and Payments column and the Income and Expenditure column should add up – starting with the Balances Brought Forward figure, add Precept and Other Income and deduct Staff Costs, Loan Interest/Capital Repayments and Total Other Payments (shown in brackets): the result should be the Balances Carried Forward amount.

In the Income and Expenditure column, the balances brought and carried forward represent the council's funds at the beginning and end of the year. This will be the total of the General Fund and all other funds – Earmarked Reserves, Capital Reserves, etc.

The Balance Sheet would look like this:

Current Assets		
Cash	45,527	
Debtors	800	
Payments in Advance	200	
Stock	380	
	———	
		46,907
Less: Current Liabilities		
Creditors	570	
Receipts in Advance	360	
	———	
		930
		———
		45,977
		═══
Represented by:		
General Fund		25,977
Earmarked Reserves		20,000
		———
		45,977
		═══

From these figures, Section 1 of the Annual Return can be prepared as follows:

1 Balances brought forward	44,869
2 Annual Precept	240,000
3 Total other receipts	52,653
4 Staff costs	(166,986)
5 Loan interest/capital repayments	(16,394)
6 Total other payments	(108,665)
7 Balances carried forward	45,477
8 Total cash and investments	45,527
9 Total fixed assets	248,500
10 Total borrowings	136,000

These figures are obtained from:

1 to 8 – The example above.

9 – This will be the total of the current value of assets recorded in the fixed assets register.

10 – The total capital value of all borrowings, e.g. PWLB and bank overdrafts.

The Annual Return should be accompanied by an explanation of any significant variations from the previous year and a copy of the bank reconciliation at 31 March.

The Income and Expenditure Account, Balance Sheet and Section 1 of the Annual Return should also show the previous year's figures.

The Annual Return also includes :

● Statement of Assurance.

● Annual Report by the Internal Auditor.

These are discussed in detail in Chapter 7; they must be completed and signed before the Annual Return is sent to the Auditor. When the audit is complete, Section 3 will be completed by the external auditor and the Annual Return returned to the council.

This chapter has dealt with the figures to be shown in the Annual Return. It must be emphasised that councils in this group still have to prepare a more detailed Income and Expenditure Account and a Balance Sheet, as required by section 7 of the Accounts and Audit Regulations 1996.

The council has a duty to monitor its financial performance; this is done during the year by comparing the actual income and expenditure with the budgeted figures on a regular basis. After the year end, it is equally important that the financial results are compared to budget and translated into an Income and Expenditure Account and Balance Sheet, even though the statutory requirement to do so may be removed, as it proves that the books balance and helps to keep track of funds and earmarked reserves.

INDEX

Index

Index